Cultivating God's Presence is an access

the growth of 'New Monasticism', a m............ .... traditions and calling multitudes of believers into a deeper and more authentic spiritual walk. Concepts like 'rules of life' and 'spiritual disciplines' can seem intimidating but Richard Roberts has a gift for making the complex seem simple and the daunting attainable. Richard draws on his own fascinating journey of life-giving spiritual discovery and combines it with intriguing history and everyday theology blended with practical wisdom. I left this book with a clearer rationale for monastic practices and their importance for us today but, more importantly, I was inspired to pursue God's presence in a more intentional and determined way; an excellent, even essential, contribution.

Ian Nicholson, Europe Director 24/7 Prayer

If you are looking for a book that will help you deepen your walk with God and what you're coming across right now doesn't quite cut it for you, you really should try Richard Roberts' new book *Cultivating God's Presence*. Although we are already twenty years in, this is the first new book I would unreservedly call a resource for the new century rather than a run-over from the old! Richard takes a long and thoughtful look at what's come to be called New Monasticism and shows us why it could prove to be so important. Cultivating God's Presence contains strong medicine. But the approach is never anything but immensely practical. If taken by enough of us, this is medicine that opens the way to a brighter future and makes me, for one, increasingly hopeful for global Christianity and its role in the world in the years ahead.

Chris Mould, social entrepreneur & former Chair of The Trussell Trust

Cultivating God's Presence is a fascinating foray into the significance of the monastic for today. With interest in such things as spiritual disciplines, new monasticism and revival very much current, Richard looks at the central theme of the presence of God and shows us that the 'ordinary' presence of God is just as important for the Body of Christ to embrace as the 'extraordinary'. He writes with humour and takes us with him on his personal journey of discovery. This book is highly informative, but accessible to all who are unwilling for followership of Jesus to be a spectator activity.

Clive Orchard, Warden and Team Leader, Ffald y Brenin

If you want to set sail with St. Brendan the Navigator on a journey into God's presence then this is the book you're looking for. Richard Roberts has crafted a marvellous description of prayer and God's presence that is offered more as a journey than an academic exercise. He refers to both ancient and modern sources that can help the reader develop an ear for the 'almost inaudible whisper of God' by 'renewing, retrieving and repurposing ancient Celtic practices'. Dr Roberts has accomplished the difficult task of bringing the ancient and time-tested monastic traditions into an understandable and modern context. I highly recommend this book for anyone who is serious about their walk with Jesus, who is seeking a deeper relationship with Him and who is also willing to risk the reality of a personal revival in the process. This book is well-written and researched and it is also quite practical - and, in my humble opinion, should find a home in every serious Christian disciple's bookcase and life.

Bob Garrett, Overall Coordinator, The Alleluia Community, Augusta, Georgia

For Catholics or members of New Charismatic Churches alike, the desire is the same - to experience the ongoing presence of God in our day-to-day lives - beyond extraordinary experiences of His glory. Richard gives hope and detailed orientation as to how to develop a Rule of Life - according to old paths trodden by the Benedictines, the ancient Celtic monks or those from other monastery traditions. But this proposed Rule fits with the circumstances of 'normal' Jesus-disciples: those with families, a secular job and civilian responsibilities. The book is a reminder for me personally and an inspiration for all those willing and wanting to cultivate the conditions for consistent growth 'into this presence of God'. Richard outlines the elements: a Psalm-oriented prayer-life and regular 'Lectio Divina'; a rhythm of work, rest and recreation; times of 'holy withdrawal' and ongoing belonging to a committed Christian community including forms of accountability to others; the blessing of regular retreats at 'Thin Places', of hospitality and of participation in our local communities and networks.

Deacon Johannes Fichtenbauer, President of The European Network of Communities & former director of the Catholic Deacons Seminary of Vienna

'A Rule of Life is an intentional attempt to create the conditions necessary to cultivate an awareness of God's presence.' As the church in first world countries struggles to find effective ways to hand on 'faith' to the next generation, Richard's book exposes the core of the longing in every human heart. Everyone is longing for authentic relationships with believers who mirror a Church that is one, holy, catholic, and apostolic, surrendered to Jesus, in love with the Father and living lives that the apostles envisioned. *Cultivating God's Presence* will be a book that every leader will want to use to establish a foundational vision for restoring the church to its proper neighbourhood based 'discipleship ministry'! My prayer is that all renewal minded Christian leaders will use this resource to foster neighbourhood-based ecumenical houses of prayer to transfigure the cultures of our ever-changing societies. When Christians (brothers) dwell together (in the same neighbourhood) God's presence is promised and the Gospel becomes visible and attractive to the culture.

Darrell Wentworth, Founder, *Awakening the Domestic Church*

The rudiments of Christian Spirituality are well established within the history of Christianity. Each believer must find some pattern or rule that will best accommodate spiritual growth for their own walk with God. The 'New Monastic' movement helps to shed light on this most important area of our lives. Dr Roberts' new book: *Cultivating God's Presence,* is an excellent summary of the New Monastic paradigm with very helpful suggestions to embolden our awareness and walk with God. If you desire as King David said: 'to follow hard after God' (Ps.63:8) this book is for you. I highly recommend it.

Scott Kelso, President of the Charismatic Leaders Fellowship

Richard's work is profoundly biblical, well researched and thoroughly theological and yet it is accessible, very readable, non-threatening and practical because it comes from the heart. It is a must for anyone seeking to deepen their walk with God and their effectiveness in life!

John Noble, Chair of the UK Charismatic Leaders Conference (1984 -2006)

Cultivating God's Presence

Renewing Ancient Practices
for Today's Church

Cultivating God's Presence

Renewing Ancient Practices for Today's Church

RICHARD J ROBERTS

Print ISBN 978-1-8384190-1-1
Digital ISBN 978-1-8384190-0-4

The Finnian Press
36 Culverhayes,
Beaminster,
Dorset DT8 3DG.

Contents

Looking for Your presence

Looking for Your presence
It's time to seek Your face
May the windows of heaven
Open up today
Let us flow with Your rhythm
The Spirit and the Word
And pick up Your burdens
Walk the land and pray

Carrying You ... Carrying You
Into the city streets and homes
Carrying You ... Carrying You
We hear the footsteps of the Lord

Can Your heavy glory
Can Your heavy glory
Can Your heavy glory
Can Your heavy glory rest on me?

© Godfrey Birtill

'Seek the Lord and his strength;
seek his presence continually!'

Psalm 105:4

dynamic might work and to the attempt to describe how we might foster an awareness of God in our everyday lives. Such subjective experience is not easily subject to scientific scrutiny. While perhaps it cannot be weighed or measured, God's presence *can* be detected and discerned, sensed and felt.

The Promise

> For the earth **shall** be filled with the knowledge of the glory of God, as the waters cover the sea.
> HABAKKUK 2:14

I can remember singing these words in church as a young Christian. The 'knowledge of the glory of God' is a way of referring to God's tangible presence and I found this imagery both moving and exciting. It connected with a hope and yearning deep inside me, as I imagined what life would be like if every person alive were conscious of God's glory. The 'knowledge of the glory of God' speaks of a future when our awareness of the glory of God will overshadow all other realities in our lives, when God will infuse everyone with hope, saturating our neighbourhoods with the knowledge of his faithfulness and his steadfast love. I pictured what it might be like if God's presence were to be experienced in every place, the grace of God covering everything, just as 'the waters cover the sea'. This is actually a promise, which God is determined to make happen: 'For the earth **shall** be filled...' Habakkuk's prophecy of a universal experience of God's presence is similar to the promised future pictured at the end of the Bible: 'And I heard a loud voice from the throne saying, "Behold the dwelling place of God is with man. He will **dwell** with them...".' (Revelation 21:3). The term 'dwell' implies that God will be permanently present in our neighbourhood.

Biblical prophecy often places a promised but distant future alongside the possibility of a foretaste of that future in the here and now, albeit in a limited or more localised way. The experience of God's glory is not simply about the 'there and then', but *to some degree* about the 'here and now' today. The Bible frequently presents us with the tension between a future hope and a present reality. The New Testament teaching on the kingdom of God is a notable example of this. The kingdom of God is shorthand for the rule of God in our lives and in the world around us. It could be thought of as the dream of God for his creation and it points to the presence of God as King. (Matthew uses the phrase 'the kingdom of heaven' to mean the same thing as the term 'kingdom of God' used by Luke and Mark. John, who does not employ this 'kingdom' language at all, uses 'eternal life' as an equivalent phrase.)

The Parable of the Talents indicates that God's kingdom will not be fully realised until Jesus returns, so although our current experience can be powerful, it remains partial and incomplete. Jesus recounted this parable to counter the suggestion that the kingdom had already fully arrived or that it was just about to arrive; 'because they supposed that the kingdom of God was to appear immediately' (Luke 19:11). He went on to explain that it would not be fully present until the 'master returns'. The arrival of the kingdom in all its fulness will see our obedience perfected, with healing and restoration our normal experience and universal justice established. This is the promised future towards which God is shepherding all history. The kingdom of God will be experienced and realised *in all its fulness* in the future. Even so, it is already present and can be experienced *in part* even now. In the words of both Jesus and John the Baptist, the kingdom is 'at hand.' Similarly, the possibility of the earth being filled with the glory of God is both a distant hope and also within reach. Habakkuk's prophecy, the promise of God's glory, represents a future promise *and* a present possibility.

Part of our calling as the Church is to keep praying for the coming of the kingdom in our world (Matthew 6:10). We pray this with confidence, reminding ourselves that one day God's rule *will* be universal and complete, and a new age will be ushered in. When we pray 'your kingdom come', as well as having a future reality in view, we often have our present circumstances in mind (Matthew 4:17). The kingdom is nearby today and we can reach out and take hold of it.

This raises the question of what we can expect to experience when we pray for God's presence. Some might ask whether what we are really describing is simply revival under another name. Revivals are, after all, times when God is tangibly present. Is there any real difference between cultivating God's presence and praying for revival? Although essentially this book is not about revival, there is a lot to be learned from studying the history of revivals. Revivals are what could be described as experiences of God's *extraordinary* presence.

God's *Extraordinary* Presence in Revival

The process of cultivating God's presence is somewhat different, as its focus is on a *less intense but more sustained* experience of God. Revivals tend to peak and wane and rarely occur twice in the same location. In their wake, believers sometimes become revival-focused, pinning their hopes on a 'second wave' and sometimes neglecting other, arguably less spectacular, ways in which God moves. Sometimes, in fact, revivals create the right conditions for a more sustained sense of God's presence, as in the case of the Wesleyan revival - at other times the legacy of revival drains away and life simply returns to normal.

During a revival, it seems that the barrier between heaven and earth is largely removed and there are unusually intense, extraordinary experiences of God's presence. These are often time-limited as in the case of the Hebridean revival of 1949 when a period of fervent prayer was followed by spontaneous outbreaks of repentance in the community. In the words of Duncan Campbell,

> without any arrangement or expectation, in the middle of the night, men and women get up from their beds, turn on the lights, and fall on their knees, crying out to God to save them from their sins, this happened over a period of many days.

People streamed across the fields and many went to the local police station to confess their sins; the only place which was open in the early hours of the morning. These wonderful events brought new life to remote Hebridean islands between 1949 and 1952. Even further back in time, similar events occurred in Wales (1904), in Mukti in India (1905), and at Azusa Street in Los Angeles (1906) as part of a global outpouring of the Spirit at the beginning of the twentieth century. Many will also be familiar with periods in American church history called *The Great Awakenings,* beginning in the 1720s. In all these instances there was a localised *extraordinary* presence of God, which went far beyond normal experience.

The Christian statesman and author Arthur Wallis wrote a book called *In the Day of Thy Power* in which he outlined several characteristics of revival, including divine sovereignty, spiritual preparation in prayer, the suddenness of revival and its accompanying God-consciousness. As examples of the localised intense presence of God, revivals often occur when the church needs to be brought back to life from a place of deadness. Revivals literally 'revive' the church, just as CPR revives someone after a cardiac arrest, or intravenous fluids revive a child who might otherwise die of dehydration.

Revivals release the life needed to renew Christians and, in addition, sweep others into God's kingdom. At best, they also lead to care for the poor and to a renewal of missionary activity. Examples of times of revival, characterised by God's presence in remarkable and extraordinary ways, are found throughout the Bible (2 Chronicles 7:1-4; 1 Kings 18:38). On the day of Pentecost fire lapped around those who were praying and they began to speak in tongues and in Acts 4:31 we read that the fervent prayer of the church resulted in the house where they were gathered being physically shaken. As desirable as these *extraordinary* events might be and much as we might long to see such happenings in our day, revival is not the focus of this book.

Cultivating God's Presence

Although revivals do bear resemblance to the idea of *cultivating* God's presence, there are some important differences. The phrase *Cultivating God's Presence* suggests that we might somehow create the right conditions for an awareness of God's presence which is more ongoing than that experienced during a revival. This contrasts with the very specific periods of time and the highly specific locations which tend to characterise revivals. God's presence may sometimes be cultivated inadvertently through, for example, decades of prayer having saturated a particular place. It may well be that this slower and often lengthier process of cultivating conditions conducive to an awareness of God's presence has an enduring effect; revival can also produce enduring effects, but this is not always the case, and God's presence can ebb away as the revival ends.

Celtic Christians referred to 'thin places', to describe locations where heaven is consistently experienced as being especially close and God's presence is tangible. God's presence can be cultivated anywhere - our home, a favourite room or even a favoured part of a room, a retreat centre, a church or chapel may all become a 'thin place'. The process involved, although no less heartfelt, is gentler and slower than that of revival with its more intensely focused, ardent prayer and large gatherings.

Although there is debate over the extent to which *our* actions play a part in bringing about revival, it is apparent that when it comes to cultivating God's presence we do have a part to play. A further contrast is that revivals are usually dependent on one or more gifted individuals, whose fervent prayer and preaching often acts as a catalyst. Evan Roberts was a key figure in the Welsh Revival and we have only to think of Jonathon Edwards, John Wesley, William Seymour and Duncan Campbell to realise that though revival is not produced by human effort it often depends on such faithful servants to provide clear leadership for it. The dynamic of cultivating God's presence is different, as *it depends more on self-leadership*, as each person faithfully seeks God through prayer and a lifestyle of obedience. Reliance on prominent leaders can make us feel the answer lies with the action of others and this distracts us from pursuing such practices ourselves. The solution to an over-reliance on leadership is the realisation that 'the shape of the church to come' lies within each individual, as we each bring our contribution and operate collectively as the people of God.

It could be argued that an overemphasis on extraordinary happenings, such as those of revival, deflects attention from finding God in a whole range of more normal human experience. Ecstatic experiences, such as my initial sense of God presence as a teenager, act as wonderful reminders of God's grace and power, but it is necessary to move on from them, and, like Moses, in Exodus 19, we need to come down from the mountaintop. In a similar vein, the disciples had to drag themselves away from the Mount of Transfiguration, despite the temptation to remain and erect a set of shrines. Just as their impulse was to construct a sort of Museum of the Transfiguration, so today there is a tendency to endlessly revisit and celebrate any mountaintop experience. It is worth noting God's negative response even to the mere suggestion of trying to build something around experience, however profound that may be (Luke 9:33-35).

As someone wisely observed, while we do have mountaintop experiences, most of our time is spent descending the mountain, in the valley itself, or ascending the next mountain. It is sad and concerning to observe churches and even whole movements which continually seek to find ways to recreate their past experience of God, sometimes at the expense of seeking God's voice and presence for today.

However amazing our most recent experience of God's presence and however wonderful the last 'great push forward' may have been, we are utterly dependent on God's daily bread, on new and fresh manna for today's circumstances and challenges. Cultivating God's presence means embracing a form of Christian spirituality that will sustain us during the descent, the valley and the ascent, not just on the mountaintop. We could call this cultivating God's 'ordinary' presence.

God's Ordinary Presence

But they who wait upon the Lord will renew their strength.
ISAIAH 40:31

The process of cultivating God's presence has as its goal the nurturing of an ongoing, consistent experience of God in our lives, to the extent that it becomes *ordinary*, a new normal. Although dramatic experiences can and do occur when we seek to cultivate God's presence, what is commonly seen is something less spectacular, though none-the-less wonderful. *Ordinary* does not imply dull - just the opposite!

Ordinary presence and extraordinary presence are not mutually exclusive. They are a continuum, two ends of a spectrum, and both can occur at different times in the same place, but the dynamics of the two are different. Revival, extraordinary presence, tends to happen suddenly, whereas God's ordinary presence is cultivated gradually and often grows stronger over time. There are many times when it doesn't feel as if God is with us, but we can expect that certain attitudes and actions on our part will eventually renew our sense of God's presence as we 'wait upon the Lord'. God's *ordinary* presence is always a possibility, whether we are in a time of revival or are experiencing a spiritual desert.

God's *ordinary* presence empowers us, we hear God speak afresh and his word becomes the bread of life, giving us strength for the journey (Luke 4:4). We can expect renewed energy as we daily wait for the Lord, even if we have to wait for some time (Isaiah 40:31). We regain hope as we are grounded again in God's love; his presence restores our soul and little by little we gain a fresh vision of God, or to use more biblical language, we become more and more aware of his glory.

Ordinary Glory

For yours is the kingdom, the power and **the glory**.
MATTHEW 6:13

The concept of God's 'presence' and his 'glory' are related. God's glory is something we experience in prayer and worship, but it is also something we carry with us into our world. Paul tells us that as we gaze upon God's glory we are ourselves transformed and we reflect his glory in our lives, just as Moses glowed with God's glory as he descended from Mount Sinai (2 Corinthians 3:18). Glory is an important term, particularly in understanding more of how God reveals himself to us and how he brings about change in our lives.

The word 'glory' can simply mean honour or splendour, such as when we talk about the glory of a sunset, but 'glory' is used in Scripture with a more specific meaning. It frequently describes the sense of awe felt when we know we are in God's presence. One New Testament word for 'glory' (*doxa*) is used to translate the Hebrew word *kabod*. The core meaning of *kabod* is that *the invisible nature of God is made visible*. Actually, m*aking visible the invisible* doesn't do full justice to *kabod* as it is multi-sensory and can describe something that we *feel;* a sense of awe and wonder, rather than something we just 'see'. Paul even uses our sense of *smell* to describe this, as he, along with his companions, carry the presence of God with them, spreading abroad the *fragrance* of Christ (2 Corinthians 2:15). The core meaning of glory is that the intangible can be touched, the invisible can be seen, and it is linked to the biblical concept of *revelation*. Revelation means an *unveiling* so that something previously hidden by a veil is now made plain for all to see (revealed). We might think of a sculpture draped with a sheet: as that sheet is taken away, suddenly, we see clearly what was previously hidden. Glory is an unveiling of what already exists, the splendour of our King, but this splendour is often obscured from view. We need to become increasingly aware of the presence of God's glory.

In the Bible God's glory is sometimes associated with particular places, such as Mount Zion, or it can be linked to particular people, such as Moses. It is seen in extraordinary manifestations of God's presence, evidenced in the tongues of fire surrounding the praying disciples on the day of Pentecost, but in other instances God's glory, his presence, is revealed in much less spectacular ways. This brings us back to the distinction between God's ordinary and extraordinary presence. We might even miss God's *ordinary* glory if we are not attentive and the idea of cultivating God's presence is partly a quest for us to become more finely attuned to his presence.

Incarnational Glory

> And the Word became flesh and dwelt among us, and we have seen his glory...
> JOHN 1:14

The Incarnation refers to the fact that Jesus, who is God, became fully human. To know what God is like we only have to look at what Jesus was like when he walked the earth, as he embodied God's glory. John 1:18 makes the point that Jesus' followers were actively *experiencing* a revelation of God. John uses the phrase 'he has made him (the Father) **known**' and his choice of word for 'known' is instructive as *ginosko* is generally used to indicate *experiential* knowledge, as opposed to head knowledge. God's glory is apprehended spiritually, emotionally, experientially. Of course, our intellect sometimes plays a part and when, for instance, we contemplate the vastness of the universe, we can experience a sense of awe. We do not have the same access to the presence of Jesus as the apostles did, but his glory is made real to us when we contemplate his life, both the miracles and more mundane interactions. Jesus' everyday existence was often unspectacular, involving practical tasks, but even in the ordinary flow of life, he was a living demonstration of God's glory.

Many people overlooked the ultimate revelation of God's glory in the life of Jesus of Nazareth. The disciples saw it: 'We beheld his glory, glory as of the only son of the father...' (John 1:14) but the majority of people failed to recognise his glory. John emphasised that Jesus was 'God present with us' when he reminds his readers that he 'dwelt among us'. *The Message* version of the Bible brings out the meaning of dwell, hidden to those of us who are not linguists, by using the more literal translation 'he pitched his tent among us'. This would have reminded John's original readers of God's presence in the tabernacle, a tent pitched in the wilderness, where God revealed his glory to the Children of Israel. John's readers would have seen the connection; Jesus was now 'the place', the tabernacle, where God's glory dwelt, but many of his contemporaries missed this altogether. We should expect something similar as far as our own lives are concerned. As we cultivate God's presence we increasingly carry his glory: many people will miss it, though fortunately not all.

We, the Church, as Jesus' body today, are called to flesh out (incarnate) God's glory to one another and the world around us - this is the idea behind the metaphor of 'the body' used by Paul in 1 Corinthians. God was revealed *to us* in the incarnation and he is revealed *through us* as we together are Jesus' hands and feet. Both the *to us* and the *through us* can be spectacular, but more often they are not. Jesus revealed God's glory to us in spectacular ways, such as miracles, but he also revealed God's glory in more ordinary ways. This is not incompatible with the understanding that there are times when we should earnestly pray for much-needed miracles. While the Spirit is involved in everyday life, guiding and prompting us in conversations, helping us to discern spirits and enabling us to speak prophetically to our neighbours and so on, in the normal course of events it is unlikely that we will spend most of our time working miracles.

Sometimes others experience God's presence through us when prayers are answered (sometimes miraculously), though more often God is experienced through having very ordinary everyday interactions with God's people. It is important to realise that this is a natural and more spontaneous process than the forced response that occurs when we try to 'act the part'. Being transformed into his likeness is quite different from having to put on a show, which brings us to the core issue: cultivating God's presence in our lives.

The Dynamics of Cultivation

God's presence is cultivated as we live in certain ways, though it would be misleading to suggest that we can somehow guarantee God's presence by simply adopting certain practices. The use of the horticultural term *cultivate* in the title points to the possibility that while we might create favourable conditions, as when gardening, we can't force anything to grow through our own efforts.

It would be misleading to think instead in terms of *How to Establish the Presence of God,* which suggests rather that *you and I* are in control with God being treated as a sort of slot machine, obliged to respond to our efforts. Churches in the West often seek to find the key to unlocking greater spiritual effectiveness and we find programmes or techniques attractive, but, sadly, they sometimes seem to appeal more to us than they do to God.

The presence of God is not amenable to a programme, nor to a spiritual self-help manual. God is often elusive and even though we pray for his presence the Spirit is not at our beck and call. Jesus reminded us that the movement of the Spirit, like the wind, can be felt but he cannot be controlled: 'The wind blows where it wishes' (John 3:8). We cannot guarantee a certain outcome by adopting a particular spiritual practice. God appears to value his freedom, as enshrined in the name which he revealed to Moses. The Bible uses names to describe the nature of the person named and the name God chose to reveal himself to Moses at the burning bush is usually translated 'I am who I am' (Ex 3:14). It can also be translated 'I will be who I will be'. I like this second translation because, although God always remains true to his character (he is who he is consistently), he is not constrained to act in any way that is determined by our will (he will be who he will be). Strictly speaking, we, you and I, cannot establish his presence, as that would suggest we are in control of God, but we can certainly seek it.

The word *cultivating* appeals because it has some biblical resonances. In his first letter to the church at Corinth, Paul pictures himself as a gardener, concerned with planting seeds, but the key phrase to note begins with 'but': '**but** God gave the growth' (1 Corinthians 3:6). Paul 'planted' the church in Corinth, Apollos 'watered' it, but it was entirely dependent on God for its growth. God was the prime mover, even though

Paul played an important role, and it is just the same for us. I'm not the gardener in our family, but gardening or *cultivating* suggests that we *create favourable conditions for growth* and hope that the seeds and weather do the rest. We can seek to cultivate God's presence, but we are always and forever dependent on him for its fruition. We have our part to play, but we can't *make* things grow by our own efforts or willpower. *Cultivating* seems to strike the right balance between our action, which is necessary, and God's far superior ability to produce the harvest in our lives.

Good Soil

To continue the gardening analogy, it is the quality of the soil of our lives which determines our capacity to cultivate a healthy crop. The Parable of the Sower indicates that the crucial issue is how receptive we are to God's word. Each type of soil that Jesus mentioned has a different capacity for cultivation, suggesting that our lives, yours and mine, can be very conducive to growth, or not. The seed that is planted is the message of the kingdom, which is shorthand for acknowledging God's right to rule and reign in our lives. We could also think of the seed as God's presence, which is more likely to take root in our lives if we establish the right conditions.

The different types of soil Jesus described could also represent our receptivity at different periods in our lives. We all have a certain amount of clay or rocks in our soil. We are not perfect people and we do ourselves no favours by pretending otherwise. We often make mistakes, sometimes we wilfully do wrong, but we can always work on our lives, improving the quality of the soil. To cultivate plants we can improve the soil by tilling it, or by adding compost or fertiliser. Similarly, when we adopt specific spiritual practices and work them into our lives, they change us, transforming the quality of the way we live as Christians and increasing our potential for fruitfulness. Improving soil quality takes time and profound changes in our lives often occur gradually. This is where the subtitle of this book, *Renewing Ancient Practices*, comes into play. These practices improve the soil quality, enabling us to be more receptive to the presence of God. They help us in our walk with God. We walk along well-trodden paths, but sometimes, to use another gardening analogy, pathways become so overgrown that they need to be rediscovered and renewed.

2

Pathways

Walking with God

Genesis 5 traces Noah's genealogy back to Adam. It systematically records the length of life of each person concerned, the names of those sons through whom the line continued and the age at which each of the ancestors fathered the next-in-line. Enoch, however, stands out as being different from all others named. We are given few details of his life except that after his son's birth, 'Enoch walked with God...' (Genesis 5:24). He was clearly someone quite remarkable. It is as if the author of Genesis breaks with facts and figures and, with some excitement, relates how Enoch enjoyed the companionship of God as an ongoing continuous experience.

The phrase 'walking with God' conjures up a life of constant fellowship with him on the earthly journey. Enoch sought out, welcomed, and cultivated God's presence. There is an implicit contrast with Adam, who heard God walking in the garden but hid from him; Enoch responded differently and joined God on his walk (Genesis 3:8; 5:24). The description of Enoch is unusual, not least in that it ends with the enigmatic statement: 'and he was not (found), for God took him'! Enoch was a rare and precious exception to the run of the mill ancestor. Because he was the sort of person God had longed for throughout those earlier generations, he was taken into the full presence of God without ever even seeing death. Enoch's fellowship with God was never broken; his lifespan, unlike that of his forebears, was not limited to a given number of years. Rather, from the moment he commenced his walk with God, Enoch experienced eternal life, beginning right here on earth. There is a further implication in this verse, which goes somewhat beyond the limits of the text. It seems important that we are told, not that God joined in with Enoch's walk, but that it was Enoch who joined God on his walk. He walked *with God*, rather than God walking *with him*. This may seem a subtle distinction, but it is an important one. While we often ask God to join in with and bless whatever we may be doing 'to join our walk', Enoch in contrast, joined God's walk. The psalmist hints at a similar dynamic when he wrote, 'Show me **your** ways, LORD, teach me **your paths**' (Psalm 25:4). Enoch's life and walk with God raises the possibility for us of a more consistent experience of God's presence.

Jesus spoke of our having constant fellowship, a constant walk, with God. He used the metaphor of God permanently dwelling with us: 'If anyone loves me, he will keep my word, and my Father will love him, and **we will come to him and make our home with him**' (John 14:23). This is a promise of the presence of the Father and the Son, whose desire is to set up residence with us. Notice that this offer is addressed to us as individuals (him or her) and that it is open to '*anyone*'. But notice also that Jesus tells us that God's presence is cultivated by obedience to his word, so this is a conditional promise.

The promise of God's presence is not an enticement nor even a reward to keep us on the straight and narrow path. It is simply the outcome of our obedience. When Jesus spoke of keeping his word, he likely had in mind his 'new commandment' that we love another as he has loved us. This commandment was simply a reflection of the fact that when we behave lovingly towards each other we mirror God's love towards us personally. God's attitude towards us is one of self-giving love (John 3:16). God is attracted to those whose lives reflect his own life, which is a life of love in action. To use the language of Genesis 5, we walk with God when our attitudes mirror his attitudes and when our actions reflect his actions. Just as we ourselves are more likely to make friends with those who have values similar to our own, so God keeps company with us the more we live in harmony with him.

When our daily lives mirror God's attitude to us, we join with the life of the Trinity, which exists in a state of mutual love between the Father, the Son and the Spirit. The twin principles of loving God and loving our neighbour reflect the nature of the Trinity (1 John 3:1-3). While this may sound straightforward in theory, in practice the requirements of love are not always obvious. Fortunately, multitudes of others throughout history have trodden this path before us and we can benefit from their advice and guidance; their pioneering efforts have cleared the way and we can follow in their footsteps. Rather than attempting to discover everything afresh for ourselves, we can instead set out to find and tread an already proven ancient path.

Finding the Path Again

Stand by the roads, and look, and ask for the ancient paths,
where the good way is; and walk in it,
and find rest for your souls.
JEREMIAH 6:16

My early experience of the Christian faith was firmly rooted within the movement known as 'Evangelicalism'. The heart of evangelical faith is a strong emphasis on the Gospel, the Good News that Jesus died so that we might be reconciled to God (we get '*evangelical*' from the Greek for Good News '*euangelion*'). Evangelicalism emphasises the centrality of the Cross, the need for personal faith and the importance of the Bible, yet the term 'evangelical' has attracted a bad press. Even some Evangelicals themselves don't like the term because those described as 'Conservative Evangelicals' teach that spiritual gifts no longer continue to be experienced in today's Church. Also, the term *evangelical,* especially in the USA, is often associated with the Far Right, even though Evangelicals exist across the political spectrum with some prominent Evangelicals on the Left.

Some people think of Evangelicals as being fundamentalist in approach and literalistic in their interpretation of Scripture. To be evangelical, it is not necessary to believe that biblical writers were automated dictating machines used by God as remote unthinking mouthpieces, nor to believe, for example, in a literal seven-day Creation. In fact, Evangelicalism was birthed in order to distance Bible-believing Christians from such raw fundamentalism.

Despite these negative associations, I continue to regard myself as a part of a broad evangelical movement, because of the 'trinity' already mentioned: the centrality of the Cross, the importance of personal faith and a very high regard for Scripture. Because of the evangelical emphasis on Scripture, soon after coming to faith, I repeatedly read the New Testament. This grounded me in the stories of Jesus early on and continues to be a highly valued foundation for my life even now.

In the early years of my Christian life, I was under the much-mistaken impression that Church History began in AD 33 and that after making a good start, the Church was on a downward trajectory for 1500 years until the Reformation - or possibly even for 1700 years, when the Wesleys appeared on the scene. Although I had read about men, women and whole movements which seemed to keep the flame alive in the intervening centuries, I regarded these as exceptions to the rule; the rule that was the steady decline and increasing laxity of the Church for hundreds and hundreds of years. In due course, I became part of the Charismatic Movement with its emphasis on the presence and power of the Holy Spirit in our lives. So for me, Church History took a further leap forward when gifts of the Spirit were restored to the Church in the early twentieth century, beginning on the first day of the new century in Topeka, Kansas.

Exploration

The reason that I embarked upon an exploration of spirituality beyond the evangelical/charismatic fold was not because I had found Evangelicalism or the Charismatic Movement to be shallow. On the contrary, I found that both had not only depth but also contributed to my faith in marked and significant ways. Rather, the impetus to look beyond my roots was the sense that there might be something missing: important elements within other Christian traditions completely absent in my Christian experience thus far. I was aware that other approaches to the spiritual life existed and perhaps these represented ancient pathways, which would help me become more deeply immersed in the presence of God. I had small glimpses over the wall to other Christian streams and these held out the possibility of a closer walk with God, a deeper awareness of his will and a much more 'grounded' lifestyle.

Over the last two or three decades growing numbers of people, like me, have begun to investigate ancient pathways which still exist in church traditions other than their own. Finding that other Christian streams have something valuable to offer can lead to dialogue and mutual learning. This involves Catholics learning from Evangelicals and vice versa - a process referred to in ecumenical circles as 'the exchange of gifts'. For those of us within the Charismatic and Evangelical fold, this has meant an exciting and unfolding journey of discovery. We have discovered for ourselves practices, traditionally associated with monasticism, which in the language of the parable of the Sower, have enriched the soil of our lives, enabling us to cultivate God's presence more effectively. These are practices which make us more attentive, more receptive to the message of the kingdom and more keenly attuned to the presence of the king.

Many Evangelicals have experienced silent or guided retreats at a monastery or retreat centre and, having found it beneficial, now build regular times of retreat into their yearly calendar. Some have explored contemplative approaches to prayer and others have rediscovered the value of using simple liturgies in worship. Books on Catholic and Celtic spirituality, such as those by Henri Nouwen, Margaret Silf and Ray Simpson, have become increasingly popular. Ancient approaches to prayer have not only created a deeper awareness of God's presence in the daily lives of many people, but also remarkably, have enabled them to experience God's glory much more consistently than before. Usually, these new-to-us practices have ended up supplementing, rather than replacing, existing evangelical/charismatic spirituality, although a few people have been so profoundly impacted by such practices that they have sought to switch streams by becoming Catholics or joining the Orthodox Churches.

Concurrently, a somewhat parallel move has taken place within Catholic circles, although generally this has been distinct from what has been happening on the other side of the Reformation divide. In particular, there has been a renewed emphasis on the Bible, sometimes stimulated through contact with Evangelicals (to the extent that some are now referred to as 'Catholic Evangelicals'). Of course, contemplative prayer has always featured in mainstream Catholic spirituality, so does not need to be 'rediscovered'. It has, however, become more prominent and many books, videos and aids to daily prayer have been produced on topics such as Ignatian Spirituality, which employs the use of imagination in biblical meditation. In addition, there has been the development of Catholic and ecumenical communities which exhibit selected features of traditional monasticism. The European Network of Communities, for instance, currently has some 8,000 people dedicated to a common life of prayer and partnership.

Ancient Wells

Isaac dug again the wells of water that had been dug in the days of Abraham his father...
GENESIS 26:18

The reintegration of monastic spiritual disciplines into the wider church, whether done intentionally or not, is not welcomed by all. I recently read an article in a Christian magazine about introducing the practice of silent prayer into the devotional life of evangelical believers. The following month the letters section included a negative response to this idea, emphatic that the use of silence in prayer was dangerous and that it originated in the weird and wonderful world of Transcendental Meditation. I agree with the letter writer that we need to be wary of misguided attempts to import practices from Eastern Mysticism, but it has to be said that the use of silence in prayer is not, in fact, an import. The letter writer appeared to be unaware of the long history of contemplation and silence within the Judeo-Christian tradition, stretching back several millennia. Some of these historic spiritual practices have become so hidden from our sight that we forget that their origin lies in biblical Christianity.

Christian silent prayer does not involve emptying the mind, as in Eastern mystical approaches; it is intentionally focusing our mind and spirit on God's presence by adopting an attitude of attentiveness. It is becoming attuned to the Spirit. Perhaps this has some resonance with Paul's reference to prayer which consists of 'groanings too deep for words' (Romans 8:26). Contemplative prayer is, in fact, a practice that is directly commanded in the Psalms, 'Be still and know that I am God'

(Psalm 46:10). Inner stillness takes a conscious effort and cannot happen if our minds are racing or preoccupied. Actively putting aside distractions is often necessary: 'I have calmed and quieted my soul' (Psalm 131:2). Several verses in the Psalms point us in the direction of prayer which relies on listening, resting, observing - in short, what we now label as 'contemplative prayer'.

Traditionally, contemplation tends to be associated with monasticism, although the charismatic experience of 'soaking prayer' has some similarities. Similarly, 'resting in the Spirit' has some resonance with the accounts of those engaging in contemplative prayer, where God's Spirit is experienced as an enveloping and profoundly restful presence. It was not until I encountered 'resting in the Spirit' in the early 1990s, that I even began to realise the association between the intentional use of attentive silence and a tangible experience of God's presence.

Closely linked to silence is the concept of solitude, another term associated with monasticism. Solitude is potentially a very creative state, but although it involves being alone, is not to be confused with loneliness, which is a negative experience. Elijah experienced solitude during his sojourn at the Brook Cherith, as well as on the mountain where he heard God's still small voice. Solitude helps us to be more attentive to God and it features prominently in the biblical narrative.

The Desert Fathers

Because monks discovered the positive effects of time alone, of solitude, the word *monastic* was used to describe them, derived from the root word *mono*, meaning single or alone. Monasticism arose in the desert. Beginning in the third-century, Egyptian men and women sought to escape the ensnaring lure of a society which, although superficially 'Christianised', represented compromise and absence of true zeal. In the desert, they experienced solitude, silence and simplicity of lifestyle. The importance of intentional silence began to dawn on me as I read about figures such as St Anthony and those who followed in his wake, known as the Desert Fathers, with their female counterparts, the Desert Mothers. As far as I was concerned, although the ancient well of solitude and silence had been there all along, it had become blocked, so blocked that it was completely hidden from view.

The idea of the desert as a place to find God has its roots in Scripture. Moses and Jesus both spent time alone in the wilderness, 40 years and 40 days respectively, before commencing their ministries. Hosea pictured the wilderness as a place where Israel's love for God would be restored, once they were drawn away from the tinsel and shallowness of the lives which they had constructed for themselves. The desert would become a place of solitude where God would 'allure' them with words of tenderness (Hosea 2:14).

The desert or wilderness is challenging, even frightening, but experiencing it is often crucial to releasing our future; without it, we can become suspended in a superficial existence. It is only when our usual, external, supports are stripped away when we find ourselves separated from the clutter and gaudiness which surrounds us day by day, that we begin to realise what is genuinely important in life. Once the daily distractions and attractions cease, alone in silence, we become acutely aware of God's presence.

Before discovering the Desert Fathers, I had, in fact, already had a powerful personal experience of silence. I had been in a very testing situation, feeling overwhelmed and anxious, and had decided to go into a darkened room to pray silently. In so doing, God's presence became tangible and gave me renewed inner strength. Despite having had this experience, it never occurred to me to include silence as part of my prayer life - until that is, I came to read about the lives of the Desert Fathers. This held out the possibility that even today these ancient but blocked wells might be reopened so that their waters might become more readily available to us nowadays.

My interest in exploring the broad landscape of Christian spirituality began when I read about the Desert Fathers in the 1990s. I learned of their emphasis on prayer, simplicity and practical wisdom while at theological college. An essay on the Desert Fathers attracted my lowest mark for any piece of written work submitted, but the course on spirituality had a deeper impact on me than any other subjects I studied. I was also intrigued by the accounts of Teresa of Avila and her 'charismatic experiences' in prayer and was impressed by the way in which prolonged meditation on the Bible had radically changed the course of the life of Ignatius of Loyola.

The combination of the wisdom of the Desert Fathers and Ignatian Spirituality provided both a foundation and the backdrop to further exploration of Christian spirituality. In particular, I came across so-called 'Celtic Christianity', whilst at a retreat centre called Ffald y Brenin in West Wales. I was not alone in my exploration, and, although unaware of it, I was a part of a larger movement of people similarly exploring the practices of monastic pioneers such as the Desert Father and Celtic Christians.

3

Past & Present

The question of what a new form of monasticism might look like today was stimulated by my reading Ian Bradley's *Colonies of Heaven.* This excellent book describes in detail what we know of the practices and the organisation of the Celtic Church. The title comes from the way in which Celtic monks often regarded their monastery as an outpost - a colony - of heaven. They viewed the monastery itself as a foretaste of the presence of the kingdom of God on Earth, the place where God dwells. This book set me thinking about how we might reshape our spiritual lives, both individually and communally, to create a 'place' where God is tangibly present.

There are some historical issues to consider before we go deeper into our subject matter. Over the past few decades, there has been a lot of interest in all things Celtic, but the historical basis of this so-called Celtic revival has been challenged. An obvious concern is the extent to which we can be certain about a movement occurring at the start of the Dark Ages.

Some authors suggest that the claim of a distinctively Celtic form of Christianity is a romantic fiction with no factual basis at all. It seems the case that a tendency towards nostalgia is a temptation for those of us who seek to find inspiration in Celtic monasticism. In *Following the Celtic Way,* Ian Bradley recounts how his students, when asked what attracts them to Celtic Christianity, give a range of reasons, often projecting their own desires back in time. One example is the claim that the Celtic Church was more relational and egalitarian than today's church, which as we

monasticism is similarly varied, and in this case, monasticism**s** (plural) is an accurate way to describe what is a broad landscape. There is, in fact, no pure monolithic form of monasticism, ancient or new. It is also worth noting that the renewal of interest in spiritual practices within Catholicism itself has not been given a label, as New Monasticism has, despite an upsurge in numbers of lay Catholics associating with monastic orders. One example of this is those laypeople who use the Benedictine Rule of Life adapted to life outside the monastery or convent, known as Benedictine Oblates.

In addition, there are communities which may not themselves use the descriptor New Monastic and yet have adopted and employed features of monastic spirituality. Stephen Davies, in *Monasticism: A Very Short Introduction*, regards the Community at Taizé in France as an example of a contemporary form of monasticism. This Christian monastic fraternity was founded in 1940 and is known widely as an ecumenical residential community in which monastic vows are taken. It could, in fact, be included among the forerunners of the current trend towards New Monasticism.

A Grassroots Movement

Over recent decades God has been stirring up an increased desire for his presence, for authentic spirituality, in many different people and many different places. New Monasticism has been one response to this and, arguably, is part of a broader movement of renewal within the Church as a whole.

One factor related to this renewal concerns the increasing numbers of people leaving Evangelical, Pentecostal and Charismatic churches. According to Alan Jamieson in *A Churchless Faith*, such churches are commonly perceived by those engaging with postmodern culture as 'faith-limiting environments', often unable to sustain people in meaningful ways through the more complex and challenging circumstances of life. Sometimes people are dissatisfied or disillusioned with the easy or even trite answers given in the face of the trials they face. New Monasticism with its reflective, meditative approach provides more subtlety and nuance, as well as the depth and tradition which has sustained countless numbers effectively throughout the ages. It has been spread, often enthusiastically, by word of mouth, through personal example, by books and other written material, websites and, most importantly, through relational networks.

New Monasticism has depended on *ordinary* people for its growth, rather than on the anointed few. While some people disseminate relevant ideas and concepts or provide inspirational and devotional material through books and talks, there are few prominent leaders, preachers or teachers. Because of the values inherent within New Monasticism, it is not a case of relying on 'God's man of power for the hour'. This shift away from Christian celebrity culture may prove increasingly attractive to younger postmodern people, wary of those who might hold out a promise of the 'secret of success', itself a modern form of Gnosticism. There is a similar scepticism of those who attract personal following based on their charismatic personality or preaching style. Those who lead by personal example, who demonstrate integrity, are deemed more trustworthy than those with good rhetoric or platform presence.

Rather than being mediated through centrally organised programmes, the exploration of monastic practices has happened more spontaneously, as a people-movement. It has *not* constituted the latest thrust forward to revitalise denominations, nor has it been the latest strategy devised by leaders to reinvigorate churches - some traditional churches have sought to introduce monastic practices with renewal in mind, but this does not appear to be widespread. With no large conferences and featuring little in religious broadcasting, New Monasticism has flourished mainly as a grassroots movement. It, therefore, represents a genuine spontaneous movement, as opposed to something more orchestrated, such as a series of organised events, might be.

One factor in the growing popularity of New Monasticism is the desire many believers have for greater authenticity in their Christian lives. Many are grappling with contextualising the demands of Christian discipleship within everyday life, in local neighbourhoods, family or work settings. This quest represents an attempt to move beyond mere doctrinal correctness (orthodoxy) to develop a spirituality fitted for life in the secular world (orthopraxy). Charismatic and Pentecostal churches can tend to present spiritual life as a series of mountaintop experiences, where hope might be pinned on revival, on the 'next wave' or the latest teaching being circulated. New Monasticism focuses on God's presence in everyday life, in the valley, as well as on the mountaintop, and, to quote Nietzsche's famous phrase, pins its hope on 'a long obedience in the same direction'.

Renewing & Repurposing Ancient Celtic Practices

Accounts of Celtic Christianity have inspired many of those seeking to explore these ancient practices and paths. The example of Celtic monasticism has envisioned many of those who have gone on to found retreat centres or communities. Iona Abbey has long been a place of pilgrimage and the dispersed Community of Aidan and Hilda, with its headquarters on Lindisfarne, takes its inspiration from the lives of the Celtic saints. The 'Celtic Revival' has been vital to the founding of the Northumbria Community, Ffald y Brenin, the 24/7 Prayer movement's Boiler Rooms and other centres of New Monasticism in the UK.

These centres, many of which support dispersed (non-residential) communities, do not attempt to *comprehensively* replicate every aspect of Celtic monasticism but seek rather to learn from and adapt those practices that seem relevant to laypeople in our current age. As has been noted, many traditional monastic orders have also extended their reach to include those who live in 'normal society' - they enable a reworking of monastic vows beyond the monastery walls adapted to each individual's setting. As long as the essential core is preserved, such adaptation is desirable - the Celtic saints were people of their own time, so their practices have required modification to be updated and reinterpreted for today. The outcome has been a deepening of spirituality in a variety of forms that have sought to capture the essence of Celtic monasticism.

The Celts lived in harsh times and this was reflected in their rugged approach to 'spiritual disciplines'. Few of us would wish to emulate Columba who was frequently to be found praying all night whilst standing in the freezing cold sea off the shores of Iona. While we would not imitate this exactly, we might find, however, that his example inspires us to develop a more intentional and challenging prayer life. New Monastics are not, then, direct heirs of the Celts, attempting to recapture every aspect of ancient monastic life. They have sought to *refashion* certain key elements of monastic spirituality for life today. This process is one of *retrieval,* enabling the *reshaping* and *repurposing* of ancient practices for today. The Second Vatican Council used the French word *ressourcement* to describe this type of process, which seeks to retain the spirit of the past without sticking to the letter of it.

The growing interest in monastic practices, Celtic or otherwise, is primarily a movement of *selective* rediscovery. Selected old treasures from ancient times are being restored and brought to life in new settings. Rediscovering the Celtic practice of speaking blessing to people or situations or using prayers for protection are highly valued treasures from the past - whereas we are likely to shy away from using prayers which call down curses on our enemies. This process of retrieval can, however, result in our adopting an eclectic approach to our spiritual lives, where we simply choose from a menu whatever might appeal to us personally. This form of pick-and-mix spirituality fails to capture the spirit of monasticism. Part Two is based on the idea that the essential core of any form of monasticism, including New Monasticism, is that we adopt a Rule of Life. This term describes a comprehensive set of practices which together form an integrated whole. A Rule of Life creates the conditions necessary to cultivate an awareness of God's presence.

Part Two

Signposts

'THE MONASTIC RULE OF LIFE SETS PRIORITIES, & BECAUSE IT KNOWS OUR PREFERENCE, IF GIVEN THE CHANCE, FOR THE EASY WAY OUT, IT ANTICIPATES OUR HIDING PLACES. BUT IT ALSO RAISES OUR SIGHTS TO WHAT MAY BE POSSIBLE. THIS WILL TAKE - INITIALLY AT LEAST - A GREAT DEAL OF EFFORT & APPLICATION.'

IAN ADAMS
CAVE REFECTORY ROAD

community. Similarly, a Rule gives a practical shape to biblical principles. Applying the teaching of Scripture to the issues we currently face is one way in which a Rule can help us.

A Rule is also helpful in other ways - it can act as a useful summary of the key issues that should guide us whenever we need to make a decision, large or small. It acts as a compass to help us navigate our way when faced with different alternatives. Both these factors - outworking biblical teaching and acting as an aid to making decisions - will become clearer over the course of this and the following chapters.

The Law

Employing a Rule is in keeping with a process we observe within the Bible itself. There are several sections of Scripture which provide summaries of how to live godly lives, but these often relate to specific contexts. The Ten Commandments and the Sermon on the Mount each outline the key issues to guide us as the People of God; they outline general principles, but they also relate these quite specifically to the situations and dilemmas which the original hearers faced. Over time we face new situations. Jesus stresses the same principles contained in the Law of Moses, but he reinterprets them for his day (Matthew 5:17-20).

Our context is different and the principles contained in Scripture need to be applied to our own setting. The temptation to set up a wooden idol in our home, or being forced to carry a soldier's pack for one mile, are unlikely to be issues facing us in the West (Exodus 20:3; Matthew 5:41). A Rule looks for modern equivalents and addresses how we can respond in a godly fashion (we might, for instance, identify our modern addiction to possessions as an equivalent of idolatry and realise that generosity is a key component of our Rule).

This begs the question as to what we mean by general principles and what they are based on. The teaching contained in Scripture centres on the understanding that we are created in God's image. As a result, we only function well when we ourselves reflect God's nature in the way we choose to live. For instance, the Old Testament repeatedly emphasises that faithfulness is deeply embedded in God's nature. We are to reflect this in our own lives so that faithfulness characterises our relationships with others. The Ten Commandments describe faithfulness in two statements: one emphasises faithfulness to God, having no other gods besides Yahweh; the second relates to faithfulness in marriage. God's faithfulness is meant to give shape to our own lives and the practical outworking of this is communicated in a summary form in Exodus 20, using short pithy statements. The remainder of the Law (Torah) can be seen as a commentary on this, earthing the core teaching given in outline form in the Ten Commandments. The Law helped ancient Israel to contextualise these commandments in the different situations they were likely to encounter. (In addition, there are sections of the Torah which deal with religious ritual). We could say that the Ten Commandments functioned as a summary of a Rule and the rest of the Torah expanded on this summary as the Rule itself.

The Psalms indicate that Israel felt a great sense of privilege in having been given the Law, their Rule. The Torah was designed to be life-affirming and obedience was not experienced as oppressive or burdensome. It was not something they resented - they didn't obey it in a 'legalistic' fashion, to earn God's favour, as is sometimes suggested. They were, rather, full of gratitude for these words of wisdom from God, overjoyed that they had been given their 'Rule' because it formed a handbook for fruitful living. Their joy is expressed vigorously in Psalm 119 where the Law is repeatedly seen as a positive blessing, helping the psalmist to live well and to thrive. The New Testament writers also provided clear guidelines for living, tailored to address the prevailing issues, and based primarily on the teaching and example of Jesus.

The New Testament

Jesus' most concise summary of the right way to live emphasised that we should act in ways which express our love of God and of our neighbour. That is an extremely succinct summary of how to live, akin to a Rule of Life and, like all such summaries, it is easy to remember. He gave an expanded version of this 'Rule' in the Sermon on the Mount, explaining in much greater detail how love for God and neighbour is outworked in a variety of situations. We should also notice that his teaching often employed hyperbole and metaphor, which leave a lot of room for us to inspired by monastic spirituality, will outline a set of practices which, like the Rule of St Francis, help us express our understanding of the heart of the Gospel in the way we live day by day.

A Rule needs to avoid being merely a set of aspirations. It has to be very practical in the way it describes how particular aspects of the Gospel are outworked. We can see this principle operating in the Rule of Benedict which places a high value on humility. This is a characteristic needed to help ensure the smooth running of any community but is firmly based on Jesus' teaching that in God's kingdom the first will be last and the last will be first (Matthew 20:16), as well as on many other of Jesus' sayings. In this way, the Rule is a form of lived, or practical, theology. Whenever a decision was being discussed, Benedict encouraged everyone to hear the opinion of the least and most recent member of the monastic community. This was not simply a pious gesture as it was based on his practical experience that often the 'last' were indeed favoured by God: 'The reason why we have said all should be called for counsel is that the Lord often reveals what is better to the younger' (Rule of Benedict 3:3). This advice helped the older members of the monastery to resist the temptation to talk too much, a sign of pride. The Rule was practical in that it provided guidelines for the monks to assess whether a meeting was good (listening to all) or less than good (listening only to the talkative few). This guide to humility-in-action is a way of living the Gospel principle mentioned above - in the kingdom of God the first (the eldest) are last and last (the youngest) are first.

As already mentioned, living the Gospel is sometimes referred to as orthopraxy (meaning right practice). There is the danger amongst all Christians that the importance of Christian doctrine (orthodoxy) is stressed to the neglect of practical discipleship (orthopraxy). It may be an overstatement to say that it can seem as if what we believe is more important than how we live, apart perhaps from in a few areas, such as that of sexual morality, where lifestyle is considered a key issue. A Rule, on the other hand, has very little to say about specific beliefs. By prioritising action it could be thought to disregard doctrine, but that would be a misunderstanding. Traditional monastics would have been orthodox in their beliefs, and many a medieval monk experienced interrogation during the Inquisitions to ensure that this was indeed the case!

A Rule of Life is not what we might regard as academic theology, but it is firmly based on sound practical theology. For the New Testament writers doctrine was never regarded as a set of intellectual ideas; it was more of a reflection on their experience of the person of Christ. Paul's letters illustrate the fact that the intended outcome of this reflection is not that we acquire a purely theoretical understanding of God. His reflections on the nature of God and on what he has achieved in Christ always has implications for how we live out our lives. Every area of life is affected by our knowledge of God with no sacred/secular split where life is divided into God-stuff and life as lived in the marketplace. In much the same way, monasticism avoids the separation between the spiritual and the secular, between belief and action. There is none of the tendency to think of what we believe as being a private matter divorced from how we act. Monasticism reinforces the fact that mundane tasks are as much the arena for experiencing God's presence as are miracles. There is no division between beliefs (theology) and our daily lives so that essentially, they belong to the same realm.

The central characteristic of good theology is that it keeps the love of God at the forefront of our thinking, but at the same time acknowledges that God is our judge. That does not mean that he is judgmental - always looking to trip us up. He does not have a pathological focus on sin, despite the impression we may get from some of our well-established liturgies. The term 'judgment' is another way of expressing the good news that justice will be done in our world. We can overemphasise grace, making God seem indifferent to evil. The inevitability of God's judgment is in fact comforting, knowing that he will eventually put all wrongs to right. Without justice every act of selfishness, abuse and failure to love our neighbour would go completely unchecked; without justice, we would exist in a universe where God allows wrongdoing to pass without comment or repercussion and there would be no real consequence to the moral tone of our actions.

The Good News is that, even when we mess up badly, there is always the possibility of forgiveness and a fresh start, which requires that we have a genuine change of heart. Good theology keeps both the love and the judgment of God in view, balancing mercy and justice. However, in most of our interactions and dealings with our neighbours, thoughts of judgment are best kept firmly in the background. As with Jesus, our main focus, our mission as the People of God, is how we might express the love of God to those around us (John 12:47).

Yet it is not always easy to describe what love requires in concrete situations. We are often faced with a myriad of choices and it can be difficult to assess competing perspectives and factors to decide between alternative courses of action. A Rule is a practical way of keeping the love for God and love for our neighbour in the foreground. It identifies the nature of our priorities before we meet different situations and this can help us choose the best course of action. A Rule describes what obedience to Jesus looks like in everyday life. Although it cannot prescribe a detailed course of action for every circumstance we might meet, it can act as a signpost, prioritising certain alternatives, pointing us towards the best path.

A Rule as Lived Values

Another lens through which to examine the nature of a Rule of Life is to use the language of 'values'. The word 'Rule' can seem alien to us today and we might more naturally speak of having particular values which help to guide our actions. The specific practices contained in a Rule are not chosen arbitrarily. They are selected because they are the practical outworking of a particular set of values. These values might be stated explicitly, or they can be implicit in the actions described in the Rule. As in a marriage or a family, having shared values facilitates the smooth running of any community.

A clear statement of values helps an intentional community, such as a church or a missions agency, to communicate its priorities to existing and potential members. It is even better if the values can be articulated as a set of practices, as this clearly indicates what is expected of members, even if the values and practices are not formally labelled as being a Rule. This can help circumvent the common experience whereby, for example, someone joins a church with assumptions about the way it operates, but after some months or years becomes disillusioned with the reality. Someone might, for example, join a church where the focus is on equipping members to be effective disciples in their everyday lives, in their families, at work or with their neighbours. If this is clearly stated it can prevent the situation where a new member comes to feel that the church is deficient in, for example, the area of running projects (or 'ministries') once he or she realises that the church has little intention of doing so. To have a Rule or its equivalent (such as a clear statement of values and how these are outworked) is better than having to slowly deduce what is actually prioritised by a particular community.

Articulating Our Values

We all hold to certain values, even if we cannot clearly articulate them. Often, we come to share the values of those with whom we have close contact. The drawback of using the term 'values' is that we can easily think we are talking about our aspirations, rather like New Year's Resolutions, good in theory but unlikely to happen in practice. Many people value honesty but those same people may not adopt the practice of filling in a customs form accurately when coming back from abroad. Another likelihood is for us to give assent to certain values signalling that we are virtuous people but without practical action to back up what we espouse.

The philosopher John Dewey pointed out how we might avoid these pitfalls. He championed the idea that we should think of our values not as a set of abstract aspirations but as those things we clearly value. For Dewey, our values are evident in those things we cherish and seen in the way we already live. Values are literally 'what we value now', clearly evidenced in our everyday choices - those things a visitor from Mars would observe if he looked at how we spend our time and money. We are values-driven and it is likely that we are drawn to a particular Rule because it is a practical expression of those things we already highly value.

I recall doing a 'values sort', a method of self-exploration, when I was training in psychotherapy. We were each given about 50 squares with different words or phrases written on them, such as 'reputation', 'having meaning in life', 'fashion', 'friendship' and 'earning money'. We had to arrange these squares in several groups, according to how important they were to us. This was not done to judge whether our values were altruistic, selfish or ethical. We simply had to try to be honest with ourselves and arrange these items in some sort of hierarchy, according to their importance to us. The aim was to become more self-aware. I learned that fashion was low on my list of values, as my friends can certainly attest, but that having a meaning in life was a high priority. My values were expressed in the way I lived: I spent relatively little on clothes but invested quite a lot of money and time into exploring the personal meaning of my faith.

The values underpinning the practices outlined in this book are often implicit, rather than explicit. The approach taken is to look at the example of the Celts and other monastic movements and to consider which elements we might re-appropriate for today. The values which underlie specific monastic practices are discernible to outsiders as well as to us - their approach to travelling strangers, for instance, is characterised by the value of hospitality.

A Rule as Monastic Rhythm

Learn the unforced rhythms of grace.
MATTHEW 11:29 (THE MESSAGE)

The final lens through which to examine the concept of a Rule is the idea that we can develop a set of interlocking practices which together form a way of life. This is the main approach adopted in this book. The term 'interlocking' is important, as there needs to be a healthy tension between action and more contemplative practices. Together these practices give rise to what might be termed a monastic rhythm.

I have played guitar in several bands and the musicians who get most acclaim are the lead singer and the lead guitarist, particularly if the guitarist plays dazzling solos. The rhythm section, consisting of the drummer and bass player, is rarely in the spotlight unless they get the rhythm wrong, and then everyone notices them. They get much less credit than they deserve. But if a band fails to keep to the beat and maintain good timing the whole thing sounds a mess; the rhythm section is actually the foundation of the band. Having occasionally played with less experienced drummers, I can attest to how vital it is to maintain a good rhythm.

Rhythm is crucial in all aspects of life. The steady rhythms of our heartbeat and breathing sustain physical life. The rhythm of the seasons determines the farming year, even though we may be less aware of this in the West where crops are sometimes grown in artificial conditions. When biological rhythms go wrong or when agricultural rhythms are disrupted by drought or too much rainfall, dire consequences result. Similarly, to function well, we also need a daily rhythm to our lives. If that rhythm is lacking we become unproductive and listless, as rhythm is needed to bind together the various elements in our lives into a harmonious whole. In fact, the quest to find a new and more productive rhythm for our lives may well lie at the heart of our interest in monastic inspired spirituality. Our spiritual lives require good pace and good timing. Jesus emphasised this when he talked about our being yoked to him to learn a new rhythm. He stressed that his yoke is liberating, not oppressive, an alternative to being 'heavy laden', or 'weighed down' as we might say today (Matthew 11:28-30).

A common practice in the days of Jesus was to yoke a young and inexperienced ox to an older more experienced one so that the younger animal gradually imbibed a good working pace and rhythm. This rhythm would gradually become its own as it learned from experience that the older animal's pace was comfortable. The younger ox represents us, yoked to Jesus as we 'learn the unforced rhythms of grace'. We start to live according to his rhythm as we walk with him - we imitate and adopt his ways and they gradually become second nature. We discover that his yoke doesn't rub and fits us well, which is the meaning of the term 'easy' in Matthew 11:29. Our new rhythm does not chafe so we feel at ease when we maintain the pace we have learned to adopt. Learning a new rhythm is a way of talking about discipleship. Disciples are apprentices, yoked to Jesus, discovering new and productive ways to live, adopting the ways of our master. Benedict's Rule had a similar aim, as it was designed to teach us to live according to an unforced rhythm of grace.

Several current authors have identified that understanding the nature of discipleship is a key issue that will determine the future of the Church in the West. I have read several books on this topic: some emphasise mentoring as key, some small groups and others recommend a deeper engagement with the Bible. These are all important elements, but they can lack an integrating framework, such as that provided by a Rule of

Life. This seems an obvious omission from the discussion concerning discipleship because, for hundreds of years, Rules have been a primary means of personal formation in the way of the Gospel. They encapsulate workable rhythms for living; the habits we develop to outwork our faith in ways that are sustainable over the long term. Adhering to a Rule of Life ensures that our rhythm includes regular times when we return to the presence of God in prayer, creating a balance of work and worship.

Becoming Second Decision People

The case has been made that a decision to live by a Rule is central to a well-rounded contemporary form of monastic inspired spirituality. Exploring a New Monastic Rule involves investing time and resources in particular practices to test it out before a clear commitment is made. Assuming we find it beneficial, attachment to the Rule grows. In traditional monasticism, those who wish to explore the possibility of becoming a monk or nun spend some years as a novice, a period when they experience monastic life first-hand before making a final decision. This is a way of testing their call and we might expect that those with a genuine call will grow stronger in commitment to the monastic way during this period. The act of investing time and effort itself can strengthen the novice's resolve. The very fact that we make an investment produces emotional attachment: 'for where your treasure is (where you have invested your resources), there your heart will be also' (Matthew 6:21, brackets mine).

Sometimes we think we need to have 100% clarity before embarking on this sort of exploration. The reality is that this is rarely achieved. Clearly, a Rule has to be attractive in the first place for us to be motivated to explore it, but it could be a mistake if we delay an exploration until we feel totally convinced. The possibility of adopting a Rule in the longer term is reinforced every time it has a positive impact on our well-being or on the lives of others. Because of this virtuous circle, we can begin tentatively to follow a Rule and to experience its effect on our lives. The practices contained in a Rule are self-reinforcing and over time they become more firmly embedded in the core of our being. Commitment to a Rule grows as we sense that these practices have resulted in our developing a more authentic and consistent form of discipleship. Commitment also increases as we experience a greater sense of God's presence through our Rule.

Deciding to adopt a Rule is a 'second decision', a further step beyond the more fundamental decision to be a follower of Jesus. Incorporating one or two individual monastic practices is different from our becoming 'second decision people' (a phrase I came across in the writings of Dr Sam Metcalf). We could, for instance, find it beneficial to follow the monastic practice of having a rhythm of daily prayer in its own right but adopting a Rule is more all-encompassing; a complete way of life representing a particular approach as to how we might live out the Gospel. A second decision involves a commitment to particular values or practices of the monastic order as outlined in their Rule, often summarised in the form of what today would be called a 'strap-line'.

Concise Guidelines

The Rule of St Francis contains one of the most well-known straplines. His summary of the Franciscan way of life was described concisely in the following way: 'The rule and life of the Minor Brothers is this, namely, to observe the holy Gospel of our Lord Jesus Christ by living in obedience, without property and in chastity'. This is often shortened to poverty, chastity and obedience, describing, in a nutshell, the life of a Franciscan friar. This is seen as imitating Christ, whom the Gospels present as forgoing marriage and living in voluntary poverty, relying on the provision of God and the generosity of others for his daily bread. It was expected that every Christian would have decided to follow Christ, but that some would become second-decision people, adopting these more radical expressions of discipleship. Francis saw his order of friars as a means of renewing, or to use his phrase 'rebuilding', the Church. The movement known as 'New Monasticism' will only lead to renewal if it invites us to make such a 'second-decision' - to voluntarily adopt an integrated set of practices designed to enable us to become better followers of Jesus.

To be of practical use, guidelines need to be few and they need, as with the Franciscan Rule, to be memorable. It is necessary for us to internalise them and to recall them easily, without having to look them up. This is the genius of the memorable Franciscan trinity of 'poverty, chastity and obedience'. Benedict's Rule also has three cardinal features summarised as stability, obedience and conversion. Stability indicates perseverance, expressed primarily in a lifelong commitment to remain in the same monastery with a particular community of monks; obedience indicates a willingness to embrace God's will, particularly his will for a particular Benedictine community, under the leadership of an abbot or abbess. Conversion is more difficult to define, but it suggests a process of personal change leading to growth in character, with increased conformity to the monastic life as its goal. Benedict's Rule is also summed up in the short phrase: work and pray, describing the main components of the monastic day. In the text of Benedict's Rule the underlying values are often implicit rather than explicit, but the strap-line functions as a concise guide, outlining the main reference points for their way of life.

A Rule functions much like the stars did for mariners in ages past, helping us to gain our bearings and navigate our way in life. We have to work through the implications of a Rule whenever we encounter a major challenge or an opportunity, but we have a compass to guide us. Our individual context determines the outworking of a Rule which gives only an outline of the main areas to consider with considerable flexibility and variety as we apply it to our own circumstances. The Rule acts as an outline in the same way that an artist might first draw an outline of something he intends to represent artistically. Once in place, the outline can be developed and filled in with any number of different mediums and in many different styles to produce an individual and unique piece of work. Starting with an outline will have given the work definition before the more creative process commences.

Classical monastic Rules are, in fact, often quite detailed with considerable definition as they are designed for closed residential communities. In such situations, there is more scope to cover most areas of life in detail and routines can more easily be prescribed. Benedict wrote 73 short chapters encompassing the issues commonly encountered in a monastery, ensuring the smooth running of a closely-knit community. However, most of us are not living in residential Christian communities so it seems more appropriate for us to use the underlying values to create a broad framework. Most New Monastic Rules are much less specific and detailed as our particular circumstances, with their unique opportunities and limitations, will shape its final form. Their outworking in specific practices depends on factors such as whether we are living alone or in a family, whether we work or study or are retired, the location and geography of where we live, as well as many other social and cultural factors. Because circumstances vary so much it can be helpful to discuss how we implement our Rule with another person, such as a spiritual director, friend or partner, to tailor a Rule to our context.

—

The following section is the outcome of my journey over many years in seeking to find a suitable Rule of Life. It explores selected aspects of monastic life and considers how these might be helpful pointers for us today. The main focus is on Celtic monasticism, but other strands of monasticism are also included. How these might shape an actual Rule is outlined in section four, where a 'sample' Rule is described and examples of how these practices might be actualised are given as illustrations to aid thinking. Examples are not intended to be prescriptive, as there are many ways in which they can be practically outworked.

A Rhythm of Prayer and the reading of Scripture is one important aspect of a monastic rhythm, and as such, is considered first, as it is the glue which holds together all the other facets of a Rule.

Part Three

The Contours of Monastic Life

CELTIC MONASTICS LIVED ACCORDING TO CERTAIN GUIDELINES DESIGNED TO HELP THEM ACHIEVE A RHYTHM OF PRAYER, WORK & REST. THESE GUIDELINES & RHYTHMS, SUMMARISED IN A RULE, SUSTAINED THEM BOTH AS INDIVIDUALS AND AS COMMUNITIES. A RULE OF LIFE PROVIDED THEM WITH CLEAR BOUNDARIES AS WELL AS GUIDING DIRECTIVES. RATHER THAN RESTRICTING THEM THIS ACTUALLY FREED THEM TO BECOME THE SORT OF PEOPLE GOD WANTED THEM TO BE.

LIKE THEM, WE NEED TO FIND AN INTEGRATED SET OF PRACTICES OR PATTERNS FOR LIVING, WHICH WILL ENABLE US TO DWELL IN GOD'S PRESENCE & TO BE CONTINUALLY RE-FORMED IN HIS IMAGE.

6

Prayerful Attentiveness

Monastic Rules are designed to balance various areas of life - work, prayer, hospitality, community meetings, rest, relaxation and so on - by prescribing and allocating particular times for these activities, creating what might be described as a monastic rhythm. For those of us living outside the monastery, our freedom to develop such a rhythm can be limited by other demands, but even so, we are still able to create some form of balanced routine to sustain us day by day. The components of this monastic rhythm are foundational, the glue which holds together the other aspects of a Rule. Establishing regular practices is vital because in so doing habitual patterns are created. These patterns eventually become second nature to us, becoming good habits which not only enrich our own lives but also enrich the life of our church or community.

A rhythm of prayer and Bible reading is a key ingredient in developing an overall monastic rhythm. It is important to realise, however, that a Rule consists of more than just a rhythm of prayer. Sometimes people (and organisations) confuse having a rhythm of prayer with having a rhythm of life, something which arises from having a Rule.

A Rhythm of Prayer

A Rule of Life is founded on a rhythm of prayer since prayer is the main way in which we continually refocus on God's presence. Celtic monasteries were centred on a rhythm of prayer and Benedict's Rule involved prayer 8 times a day.

At the beginning of my Christian life, I prayed and read the Bible each day, usually in the morning. After a few years, I heard some teaching which suggested that this was a form of legalism, so I decided I would give up having regular prayer times. 18 months later I realised that my relationship with God had become cursory. I concluded that daily prayer, though not 'a law', was actually helpful. I re-instituted my former practice of praying once a day, which proved beneficial and helped me have a much greater sense of God's reality. The downside of this morning routine was that, although it grounded me in God, the effect faded as the day wore on. I needed to find a more sustaining rhythm of prayer.

I came across the idea of praying several times a day in the late 1990s, but it became a necessity in the mid-2000s when difficult circumstances left me in a low state emotionally. I was drained spiritually and felt burnt out, having juggled a part-time career alongside leading a church for over 20 years. I had never taken a sabbatical to recharge my energy and enthusiasm. I needed to find rest in the presence of God and return to that place of rest several times during the day.

During this rather desolate period, spontaneous prayer was near impossible - instead, my wife and I used the set prayers and liturgy in *Celtic Daily Prayer*, produced by the Northumbria Community. This was a lifeline. There were prayers to use each morning, lunchtime and in the evening, with Bible readings and meditations - some of the prayers were Scripture verses and repeating them each day grounded me in the truths they conveyed. We managed to survive this difficult prolonged interlude with *Celtic Daily Prayer* helping us to refocus on God, but without having to dwell on our own situation too much, something which would have resulted in a rapid downward spiral.

Before that time my approach to prayer was that it was mainly about intercession, letting God know our requests. This is clearly important, but perhaps a broader view of prayer was needed. Prayer can be a way of focusing our attention on God, becoming increasingly aware of who he is and what he has done for us. It is as much about *our being attentive to God* as it is about expecting him to be attentive to us. Regular prayer helps develop such attentiveness, but the circumstances of life are such that it is not always easy to find the time or to feel motivated to pray. This is where a rhythm of prayer, as part of a Rule, may help us.

Praying the Psalms

The Psalms featured highly in the prayers of Celtic monks, who often recited 50 psalms each day and, in some cases, the whole of the Psalter, consisting of 150 psalms. They memorised them and as they recited them, something which we may tend to shy away from, they used the psalms to address God, making the psalmists' words their own and giving shape to their praise. The prayers and songs of the psalmists, however, encompass more than just praise. While today the Church at large tends to favour Psalms of Praise, the most common form of psalm is the lament. Our favouring praise is understandable, since using lament in prayer can be disturbing, bringing our sadness or anger into consciousness; not always a comfortable experience.

In addition, there are sections of the psalms which call for revenge on our enemies (the so-called 'imprecatory psalms'). These particular passages do not sit easily with us because we know that Christ calls us to forgive, rather than seek revenge. Some people even tend to regard these sections as being 'sub-Christian' literature, easily abandoned in the light of the Gospel. But these psalms are vital because forgiveness is often a process rather than a one-off event. This process only really begins once we acknowledge that we feel people have actually wronged us. Unless we acknowledge these feelings, forgiveness remains a superficial attempt to overlook the past and its ongoing effect on us.

Jesus told Peter that he had to forgive his brother 7x70 (490) times (Matthew 18:22). I used to think Peter's hypothetical 'brother' had sinned once and then gone on to commit 489 further sinful acts to make up the full 7x70 - perhaps Peter had to forgive each of the 490 wrongs in turn. I now read it differently, based on the experience that some individuals repeatedly come to mind when I pray 'we have forgiven our debtors'- referring to those who have 'trespassed against us' in the words of the 1662 version of the Bible. Reciting those passages in the Psalms which talk about 'our enemies' can bring unexpected people to mind. We can be unaware of deeply buried hurts, or of our wariness of a particular individual, or of the need to forgive someone for something they have said or done. Only when we realise how we really feel, can we release them from their debt to us, bring them to God and pray for their blessing. Try praying the Psalms and you will see how this process is effective in freeing others and ourselves from the prison of unforgiveness.

Sometimes we need to forgive an individual well over 490 times (I am just as certain that we each feature in the prayers of others as being the one in need of forgiveness 490 times). Each prayer of forgiveness is genuine and effective, but soon the old grudge creeps back in again. I need to pray again 'forgive Bill who trespassed against me' (Bill is not a real person, in case you are called Bill and I know you). Eventually, Bill no longer features in my prayer; the work of forgiveness has been completed as the 490+ prayers have completed their task. Having to repeatedly pray forgiveness can feel like a weakness on our part but it is necessary - deep forgiveness needs us to be honest about the part we believe someone has played in our past. This is a way in which we can refresh our soul, clearing away the clutter of resentment from our inner world. We sometimes need the robustness of the psalmists' words for us to connect with those feelings which we don't want to admit to ourselves or God.

The ancient practice of praying the whole of the Psalms had many advantages over a more selective use of the more encouraging passages, including the fact that it can help forge a robust relationship with God. By including all the psalms we follow the example of ancient Israel in viewing *all* of life, the good, the bad and the ugly, as appropriate to bring before God. This creates a more holistic and integrated approach to Christian spirituality, perhaps a more realistic and less 'sanitised' spiritual life. It also has the effect of soaking us in Scripture, a highly valued experience discovered by anyone who has taken part as a guest in the daily prayer rhythm of any priory, friary or monastery.

Lectio Divina

Using Scripture as the basis for prayer is a good practice. Laura Swan, in her book *Engaging Benedict*, reinforces the foundational nature of prayer and Bible reading, suggesting that it was the 'primary curriculum' of the monastery. This is an important point for those of us who wish to develop a Rule for today. A monastic-inspired rhythm needs to include a pattern of spiritual reading, especially Scripture. Prayer and Bible reading naturally go together and there is a synergy between these two activities: what we read can naturally lead us to pray and our prayers are sometimes answered as God speaks to us afresh through Scripture. This synergy became formalised after the time of the Celts, as an effective means of integrating Bible reading and prayer and so creating the monastic practice of Lectio Divina (Latin for 'divine reading'). It is, in fact, a method that relies on our being attentive to whatever God might be highlighting to us through Scripture - but Lectio then goes beyond mere awareness and helps us to turn our insights into prayer. It starts with reading, but its aim is prayer (and action).

Lectio Divina involves four stages: first, we read the passage, seeking to understand its most straightforward meaning (reading and thinking); next, we slowly chew over the passage, focusing on any section that catches our attention (meditating); then we pray, bringing to the Lord any people or situations that have come to mind as we meditated on the passage (speaking); finally, we have a time of silence in God's presence (contemplation). The first stage (reading) is the same process adopted in a traditional Bible study, where an understanding of the plain meaning of the text is sought, while the subsequent stages make us more open to hearing God speak to us personally through the passage. Lectio is a good way to hear God afresh and I would recommend it as an alternative to traditional Bible study.

Lectio also differs from more structured cognitive approaches where we seek to think through the practical application of a Bible passage (sometimes known as a Discovery Bible Study). Lectio relies on the Spirit rather than our own analysis and application to highlight the particular areas we need to focus on. Both approaches have their place and both can be helpful, but with the renewal of ancient monastic practices in mind, Lectio is perfectly suited for the purpose of listening to the Spirit as he speaks to us through Scripture.

It is worth following the stages of Lectio Divina as a *formal* practice for some months, going through each stage deliberately, until it becomes a habitual way to approach Scripture. After a while, we find we instinctively spot the verse that jumps out from the page and catches our attention and in time we naturally turn our meditation on the passage to prayer. Reading Scripture in this way has many beneficial effects: it increases our awareness of the presence of God; it sharpens our ability to hear God; it increases our capacity to receive new light and it helps us to see old truths reframed as we gain fresh insight into their relevance for our lives. Lectio can easily be done in a group, initially sharing knowledge and observations in conversation together and then utilising group silence at the meditation stage.

Attentiveness

> In one sense all monastic practices are geared towards creating that ear that is attentive to the still small voice.
> SIMON O'DONNELL (THE OBLATE LIFE)

A powerful interaction between prayer and Scripture reading occurs when we develop a posture of attentiveness. When we read and pray with an ear to what the Spirit might be saying to us, we have a two-way dialogue, rather than simply a case of *our* speaking and God hearing *us*. There is a place for the latter in intercession and our speaking blessing, for example, but listening, attentive prayer is perhaps more fundamental to our spiritual health. Practices which foster attentiveness realign our lives to the reality of God's presence and this is essential when life is particularly pressured or stressful. Prayerful attentiveness also sharpens our awareness of God in times other than when we are praying, in everyday life, when we find ourselves more attuned to the wind of the movement of the Spirit. Being attentive to God enables us to gain fresh vision; we are realigned with his will for our world and our individual lives. It creates the opportunity for the Spirit to impart fresh life so that we are renewed and inwardly re-formed in his image.

When we listen to God we also become aware that he is already active in situations before we even ask, that any mission we are engaged with is primarily and fundamentally God's mission (missio Dei), not our own. We begin to appreciate that we are working *with* him in these situations, rather than working *for* him or even worse, independently of him. Attentiveness is acquired slowly and silence helps, particularly if we are addicted to noise (or our mobile phones).

Contemplation

As we saw earlier, silence and solitude feature both in the Bible and in the practices of the Desert Fathers. But silence can provoke feelings of anxiety within us and some of us surround ourselves with constant noise to avoid it. Rather than be alone in our own and God's company we prefer the distraction of music, a podcast or the radio to block out whatever is in our heads. Others fear that silence will open them up to forces other than God or may lead them down the path of Eastern mysticism. A detailed account of silent prayer is beyond the scope of this brief survey, but the following comments made by someone on a blog I had written on this topic during Covid 19 lockdown, tracks her journey in exploring silent prayer:

> I've just read your latest blog on silence - I love it! I used to assume that it was my schizoid/introverted tendencies which made times of solitude and silence so essential to me, but since I discovered Thomas Merton et al (courtesy of David Runcorn at Lee Abbey) and have been increasingly healed from trauma, I have found that the quality of the silence has gradually changed.
>
> As I read your post, I felt the familiar sense of inner 'spaciousness' I get - almost a feeling of being on hallowed ground somehow, while still grounded on my office chair in front of my computer. I find myself listening intently, as if to something just out of earshot that is strange and yet dearly familiar. It isn't always like that, of course - at other times the 'cage full of monkeys' in my head just won't quieten down for long enough, and Coronavirus lockdown with my husband has been particularly challenging, as he surrounds himself with a wall of noise all the time!
>
> There are also times when I feel as if I've been 'struck dumb', and literally can't find words - interestingly, it's happened several times while attending Christian counselling conferences, where the worship tends to be extremely loud and 'wordy' - I can get caught up in that as easily as anyone else, but on these occasions, I felt as if I were drowning in words, and couldn't hear the 'still small voice' anymore. It's been like that during lockdown to some extent - most of the time I'm deeply present and involved in Sunday meetings and

Tuesday prayers (except on the days when I'm struggling to stay focused), but I can't seem to find words which wouldn't sound trite and superfluous, given the gravity of the issues we pray about; it's also about the difficulty I have in speaking up in large groups to some extent, but not entirely.

The wisest words I have ever heard about prayer were from a monk (I can't even remember who, but it doesn't really matter); he said: 'pray as you can, not as you can't'. That has been a great comfort to me when my poor, silent efforts have felt so inadequate - it reminds me that it's not about me anyway!

Another term related to silence is *contemplation*. We contemplate something when we take a long and unhurried look at it. This creates a depth of engagement, a sustained focus. Interestingly, the word *empathy* was used first to describe our ability to 'get inside' a work of art and allow it to move us. Only later was it applied to our being able to appreciate the feelings of another person to some extent. One of the New Testament words for looking is *theoreo,* which means to look upon, to gaze, to ponder; we get the word 'theory' from *theoreo*. Theories emerge from the sort of contemplation that occurs when someone immerses themselves deeply in a particular topic. As we gaze upon Jesus, we gain a deeper appreciation of his presence, we become aware of his glory and this requires silence, stillness and attentiveness. We gaze upon the face of Jesus as we read the Gospels or think of his love for us or when we sing worship songs. These forms of contemplation allow the Spirit to transform us by revealing to us the glory of Jesus (2 Corinthians 3:18).

The approach to psychotherapy in which I trained was based on adopting a contemplative attitude towards clients, often requiring silence on the part of the therapist. Attentiveness was key and this meant not jumping to conclusions or fitting the person's experience neatly into some aspect of psychological theory. I was fascinated by the way in which new perspectives often emerged after months of such 'contemplative' therapy. Sometimes a crucial insight, a revelation of sorts, would occur to the client and therapist independently at the same time. This process could not be rushed. It involved actively waiting for new meaning to emerge and an openness to see things anew. This experience has some parallels with contemplation in prayer, where we allow God to reconfigure us, to reveal more of himself to us as we sit attentively in his presence.

The Almost Inaudible Whisper of God

The two great enemies of awareness of God are noise and haste...
AIDAN RYAN

A posture of attentiveness might sound easy to achieve but learning to discern the still, small voice of God is not always easy. Elijah heard God speak on Mount Horeb, but he had to listen hard, as it came as an almost inaudible whisper. The whisper of God easily gets swamped by spectacular sights, by noise, by earthquakes, wind and fire (1 Kings 19:12). The Elijah story is interesting because we read that even though God himself produced these phenomenal sights and sounds he was not 'in' them. This could suggest that seeking the spectacular might not be the best approach for us to take.

One rabbinic commentary on this particular passage describes the sound Elijah heard as the 'daughter of a voice'. This was in the days when, stereotypically, sons were boisterous and noisy, whereas daughters were much quieter. While we might feel this is an unenlightened, rather sexist phrase, the point is that God's voice is not always the strongest and loudest voice we hear. His only just discernible speaking can easily fade, unobtrusively, into the background in the face of other competing voices. We are quite distractible and can easily miss God's voice unless we deliberately develop ways to become attentive.

Of course, God's voice sometimes needs to be distinguished from our own thoughts and desires. Thoughts and feelings can also originate in the activity of malign spiritual forces. It takes time and experience to learn how to exercise the gift of discerning of spirits with any degree of skill (1 Corinthians 12:10). There is a lifelong process of learning to distinguish the source of our inner inclinations, thoughts and desires. Ignatian spirituality, beyond the scope of this book, is particularly helpful here, as it offers a tried and tested set of sound discernment processes. It is the most helpful approach to weighing our thoughts and feelings that I have encountered.

Responding to God's Voice

Because God often leads us with a whisper, his promptings can easily be missed. It is also easy to suppress or ignore the whisper of God. I sometimes have a clear inner sense that I should say a certain thing to someone, with words clearly forming in my mind and, at other times, can feel restrained from speaking; an inner check which indicates that something I had thought of saying would come across as unhelpful. I am able to ignore either whisper, usually to my regret, but I am slowly learning to take note. Some people are especially sensitive to the movement of God within. Someone might come into their mind in a seemingly random way and, from experience, there is the realisation that this is likely to be a prompting to contact them. Of course, there may be lots of reasons why a particular person comes into our mind, but when this sense persists it is often a nudge from the Spirit.

Learning to distinguish our random thoughts from God-thoughts is a life-long process. I once heard some good advice on this topic from a leader in the Catholic Charismatic Renewal. She suggested that in order to discern the source of such thoughts a test is to try to ignore them; if they originate from a malign source they will fade over time ('resist the devil and he will flee from you'), but if they are from God they will persist and will grow stronger over time. That wise advice releases us from having to give immediate expression to anything and everything that pops into our minds, just in case it is the Spirit leading us. If something is, in fact, from God it can usually wait a few days before we communicate it, so we need not put ourselves under pressure to respond immediately. The classical prophets of Israel engaged in the lengthy process of writing down their prophecies, some of which we are reading millennia later. They did not feel constrained to deliver their revelation on the day they sensed it and, indeed, it is still a fresh word to us today despite being received many centuries ago.

Discerning God's Voice

If we wish to make any progress in the service of God...we must keep ourselves in the presence of God as much as possible... If a tiny spark of God's love already burns within you, do not expose it to the wind, for it may be blown out. Keep the stove tightly shut so that it will not lose its heat and grow cold. In other words, avoid distractions as well as you can. Stay quiet with God.

SAINT CHARLES BORROMEO (1538-1584)

It is difficult for God to speak to us if we are constantly preoccupied with our concerns or even with the difficulties of our friends and families. The noise in our heads has to die down for us to be able to hear God afresh. Intercession, talking to God about our needs and the needs of others, is vital but it can become too dominant in our prayer lives, in which case we need to refocus, setting aside more time to listen to God. Isaiah described his own experience of regular attentive listening in an unusual phrase - 'having an ear that is awake': 'Morning by morning he awakens; he awakens my ear to hear as those who are taught' (Isaiah 50:4).

Our desire to know God and become increasingly sensitive to his voice only becomes a practical possibility when we develop routines involving quality time set aside to listen. Our ability to hear develops as we pray, sit in silent contemplation or read Scripture. We have to learn to 'waste time' with God. I have 'wasted' many hours looking at the surface of rivers and lakes when fishing or walking. As a consequence, I have developed almost a sixth sense that enables me to spot the presence of fish. Sometimes I might notice a barely discernible change in the pattern of the ripple on the surface of the water but at other times I am not sure what has alerted me. Or, to change the analogy, I can hear the difference between different makes of guitar when I listen to music, simply because I have spent too much time messing about with guitars and have become familiar with their different tonal qualities. Just as time invested in a hobby results in our developing certain abilities, time given to prayer and attentive reading creates a heightened awareness of the nature of God's voice.

These practices also enhance our capacity to be attuned to the spontaneous promptings of the Spirit in our everyday encounters. Time spent in stillness before God creates a sense of inner peace and increases our capacity to be attentive. We carry this with us, enabling us to become more aware of our inner world, of our spirit, and more sensitive to his leading (Psalm 131). Time invested in actively listening to God, quietly and attentively, increases our sensitivity to the Spirit at times when we are occupied with other tasks. Reading the Bible is also a great aid in developing our ability to discern the voice of the Spirit. When we read Scripture in an unhurried manner we gain a sense of the nature of the word of God. This can only be described as its feel, a sense of the *quality* of God's communication to us. This is difficult to describe precisely, but it is nonetheless real. When God whispers to us as we go about our daily business, we recognise the same 'feel', the same voice that we have experienced in our Bible reading; there is a resonance with what we have repeatedly experienced in private and we can identify the source, despite any distracting buzz around us (John 10:27).

Familiarity with Scripture helps us grow in discernment more broadly. We gain an understanding of the *parameters* of God's will as we read the Bible and this awareness provides us with *guidelines* to weigh our thoughts and feelings. In addition, a particular verse or two will sometimes stand out from the rest of the passage, *highlighting specific issues* which we might need to consider. Sometimes this points us towards a particular course of action, in which case reading the Bible is transformed from something of a duty to an adventure with God - prayer and Bible reading can become vehicles of transformation in our lives whereby God comforts, reassures, realigns and redirects us. When God uses Scripture in our lives it reminds us that he is indeed with us. Attentiveness to God can also involve our reading relevant devotional books or listening to podcasts or music, or to anything else we may find conducive to hearing God's voice. We might also set time aside to sit in God's presence to intentionally think about the direction of our lives.

Being Realistic

I have often felt daunted by the thought of developing my own prayer life, but it helps to remember that the quality of the time we spend is often more important than the quantity of time. We are likely to succeed in becoming more attentive to God if we are very realistic about our circumstances and aim to create sustainable practices; we are likely to fail and become discouraged if our aspirations are unrealistic. I began my working life as a junior hospital doctor in the bad old days of what was called a 1 in 2 rota; fortunately now done away with. This was the gruelling requirement to work every weekday and, in addition, to be on-call in the hospital every other night and every other weekend. This meant that every second week I was at home for only two nights out of seven, with over 140 hours spent in the hospital (during the alternate week I had three nights off plus the whole weekend). Sometimes junior doctors were up half the night before working the next day and, as a result, I spent most of my life feeling completely exhausted. In that sort of situation, it is impossible to stick to a definite rhythm of prayer, but it is possible to pray the Lord's Prayer each day, even if when driving or walking. Practices need to be achievable and tailored to our individual circumstances. 10 minutes of attentive, focused prayer or Bible reading in an attitude of openness to God is more valuable than 30 minutes of simply 'going through the motions'.

Attentiveness creates the space for us to hear God and when we regularly engage in listening prayer and Scripture reading we usually expect to experience his presence with us. There are exceptions to this, however, and having realistic expectations is important. The experience of Christians through the ages is that we have times when God feels absent. Recognising that this is normal can save us from feeling we have done something wrong if we are not currently experiencing God's presence.

Attentiveness is not a technique that will automatically produce certain results. There are times of spiritual crisis described by St John of the Cross in his poem *The Dark Night*. Sometimes experiences of God's absence coincide with episodes of depression or can follow a bereavement. While usually these are episodic and temporary, Mother Teresa of Calcutta experienced times of the 'dark night of the soul' throughout her entire life and much more frequently than most. These periods were referred to by Ignatius of Loyola as times of desolation; he used the term 'consolation' for the opposite experience, where we sense God's presence beside us, leading us on.

Consolation is our more normal experience as Christians and is to be expected (this is a simplified use of these terms and Ignatius was much more nuanced than my simple explanation). In general, we are encouraged to expect that God will most often not be silent or feel absent but will speak to us and direct us: 'All who are led by the Spirit of God are the sons (and daughters) of God' (Romans 8:14).

7

Pilgrimage

Attentiveness, the focus of the previous chapter, is developed by periods of withdrawal for prayer, silence and Bible reading. Ian Adams, in his book *Cave, Refectory, Road* refers to time spent alone in prayer as being in 'the cave', our equivalent of a monastic cell; the refectory refers to the time we spend with others and the road is time away from whatever we regard as our equivalent to the monastic community. Time 'on the road', when we renounce the security of the familiar, is the topic of this chapter.

Perigrinatio

Celtic Christianity viewed all of life as a journey, a pilgrimage - termed *perigrinatio*. This involved renunciation, walking away from what 'the world' had to offer, similar to the sentiments expressed in Bunyan's *The Pilgrim's Progress*. Celtic Christians saw themselves as those who were seeking another city, whose maker is God (Hebrews 11:14-16). Although it was primarily an attitude of heart, pilgrimage found concrete expression in the actual journeys made by the Celtic saints.

Life for Celtic monks involved time spent in prayer and study in their cells, time spent working alongside others in farming and time involved in providing hospitality. They might also take to the road and undertake short term mission trips, venturing into country areas to evangelise, found churches or resource existing churches.

Many famously went on much longer missionary trips where they embraced the insecurity of entering unfamiliar regions where they had no official status. This often involved considerable risk and it meant disrupting the security of the well-ordered and predictable life guaranteed in the monastery. They were more concerned with the will of God than with those things to which we become so easily attached - possessions, status, the familiar and predictable. One way in which they framed their adventures was to view themselves as being permanent exiles for Christ, living far from home.

They were not pilgrims in the sense that they were journeying to a sacred site to experience God - rather, they travelled to new lands carrying with them the presence of God, taking his presence into new territories. Celtic Christians lived on the fringes of civilisation and their contact with the outside world was often by boat. Their highway was the ocean which has always been a dangerous place and there are now more than 40,000 shipwrecks off the coasts of Britain and Ireland. The inherent dangers, such as storms or piracy, did not prevent monks from inhabiting this particular space. Their willingness to risk all for Christ is illustrated in the lives of Columba, Columbanus and Brendon the Navigator, whose journeys are wrapped in the language of myth and legend. The urge to become exiles for Christ was very strong for these Celtic saints and an impulse to venture beyond their borders gave rise to what would now be described as a missional movement.

Many of us still long, metaphorically speaking, to step into oceans deep and experience God's presence in ways we never can do whilst standing safely on the shore. This is the theme of the song *Oceans: Where Feet May Fail*. Over 120 million YouTube hits for various versions of this song suggests that it expresses a longing which resonates with huge numbers of young people in particular. Christianity presented as a safe option holds less appeal. Religion as a security blanket against a harsh world attracts few young people, and many of us who are older also fail to be attracted to this unadventurous version of the Faith. Jesus commanded his disciples to go across Lake Galilee, risking shipwreck, and the lesson for us is that we can only know the power of Jesus to intervene and see us safely to the other side if we do set out. Despite any concern we have for health and safety, the urge to relinquish our attachment to security is strong - sometimes we just feel the need to step out of the boat (Mark 5:35-41). But the motivation cannot be for the sake of adventure; it must come first from having heard God's voice to us (faith comes by hearing) and it must originate in a vision of God's glory.

The Vision of God

Here am I! Send me.
ISAIAH 6:8

Isaiah spent time in the temple, attentive to God presence, and that created the context for a spectacular vision of the glory of God. Overwhelmed by God's presence, he overheard the Trinity talking about their need for a messenger to speak to Israel. Isaiah offered himself for the position, an action which encapsulated the core of availability. He had heard the heartbeat of God and responded by volunteering to be involved but notice that he couldn't set off until he received God's 'say so'. He could not go ahead simply because he realised the need. He had to be commissioned, sent by God. This story is a challenge to the teaching, sometimes heard, that 'the need is the call'. In the Greek version of the Old Testament, the Septuagint, the verb 'send' in Isaiah 6 (*apostello*) is the word from which we get the noun 'apostle'. If we were being rather literal, we could say that Isaiah was 'apostled' by God. His willingness to listen to God and to be sent and his freedom from attachment to an easier life, was only possible because he had a vision of God's majesty. This is the only way in which we can become apostolic people and apostolic churches. Well thought through exegesis or the pressure of a recruitment drive to 'do the stuff' are no substitute for a revelation of the love of God.

I sometimes wonder how many people God has wanted to call to his service but who became distracted by some pressing need and never actually 'went up to the temple' on that day when God was strongly present. Perhaps some did go and heard the call but simply ignored it, in order to continue with life as usual; the security of the familiar can be more appealing than the challenge of the new. Perhaps life was challenging enough already without the added complication of God demanding time and attention. Before Moses stopped and turned aside to take a closer look at a burning bush, how many people were so preoccupied that they walked right past it? I wonder if there were several Ezekiels having strange visions in exile, but who decided that life was already tough enough and that becoming a prophet was simply out of the question. God's challenge to a settled existence is only effective if we hold the present set-up lightly and are willing to respond with a flexible attitude.

Flexibility

> Another of his disciples came to him, 'Lord, let me first go and bury my father'. And Jesus said to him, 'Follow me and leave the dead to bury their own dead'.
> MATTHEW 8:21-22

This hard saying of Jesus addresses our priorities and makes us consider our attachments to people and things. The request of this unnamed disciple actually seems quite reasonable. It could be argued that he was simply working out the biblical command to honour father and mother. In Jesus' day, the duty to bury one's relatives had become so important that it took precedence over all other religious commandments, so this saying of Jesus is even more striking. I feel somewhat sorry for this man, as there was even a biblical precedent for his request: on becoming Elijah's disciple, Elisha was allowed to return home to bid his parents farewell (1 Kings 19:20). Jesus seemed to demand more than Elijah, insisting that following him must take priority over all other relationships. As with several other statements of Jesus, hyperbole is used to make a point, but this saying was recorded to underline the fact that discipleship is meant to be radical - it requires that we are flexible in our attachment to things as they stand.

Pilgrimage, in the sense the Celts meant by the term, requires this sort of freedom from attachments and is a good way to frame what is expected of us as followers of Jesus. When God calls us to embark on a particular course we can usually find a good reason to be otherwise occupied. Thought of in this way, pilgrimage might require us to set out on an actual journey or it might involve a new departure, a new venture perhaps, without a change of location. Pilgrimage means that a flexible attitude is needed; it also requires us to create those spaces of prayerful attentiveness in which God can redirect us. The combination of attentiveness plus freedom from attachments is key to effective discipleship.

The early Jesuit missionaries are a great example of those who sought freedom from attachments; they were ready to be redirected 'at the drop of a hat'. They sought to cultivate an attitude of adaptability and flexibility, ensuring that their commitment to God was not compromised by attachment to anything that might hold them back. Their term for this was 'indifference'. Indifference did not mean that they did not *care* about people or projects; the opposite was, in fact, true and they sometimes cared so much that they suffered greatly on behalf of others. Their goal to cultivate indifference reminded them that the present circumstances of their lives, with all the benefits, were meant to be held lightly. They were to develop indifference to their own comfort, to their security in the status quo and relationships, which, however good or beneficial, might hold them back from obeying God's call.

'Indifference' was fostered by a forty-day retreat based on the *Spiritual Exercises of St Ignatius*, where they meditated on the Bible and biblical themes, and which created a depth of engagement with God and his mission in the world. It helped shape their priorities. Indifference allowed God to redirect their present and to shape their future. It created inner freedom which enabled a swift response to God's leading. A similar sentiment is expressed in Methodist Covenant Prayer:

I am no longer my own, but thine.
Put me to what thou wilt, rank me with whom thou wilt.
Put me to doing, put me to suffering.
Let me be employed for thee or laid aside for thee,
exalted for thee or brought low for thee.
Let me be full, let me be empty.
Let me have all things, let me have nothing.
I freely and heartily yield all things to thy pleasure and disposal.
And now, O glorious and blessed God, Father, Son and Holy Spirit,
thou art mine, and I am thine.
So be it.

And the covenant which I have made on earth, let it be ratified in heaven.

This prayer expresses perfectly what the Jesuits meant by indifference and what is meant here by the phrase 'freedom from attachments'. John Wesley was influenced by Ignatius Loyola, founder of the Jesuit order, and it is possible that the concept of indifference inspired this prayer, recited every year by those in the movement which Wesley founded. Of course, however serious our intent to follow Jesus, none of us are unfeeling and attaining freedom from attachments is often a very gradual process, completed over many years. This process is aided hugely by having a rhythm of prayer, which constantly redirects our gaze Godward and allows him to bring about the necessary change in our lives.

God on a Mission

The view of pilgrimage as our carrying God's presence with us has to be balanced with the realisation that it is not simply the case that we take God's presence with us into new situations - he is *already* active there. God goes before us in mission and is working in people's lives before any encounter we might have with them. And his action in loving the world, his priority in mission, *far* precedes any thoughts we might have had (John 3:16). The Celtic Church perhaps went some way towards this realisation, and, in the words of Ray Simpson, they identified and worked with 'Gospel-friendly trends' in the societies they evangelised (*Exploring Celtic Spirituality*). In other words, they sought to incorporate elements considered conducive to Christianity, such as certain beliefs and some existing relational networks. In recent years our understanding has incorporated this approach by highlighting the way God can reveal himself to people through contemplating nature or more directly through his Spirit, both of which were elements of Celtic Christianity.

In the 1930s a theologian called Karl Hartenstein affirmed the idea that God is already engaged in the world before we, the Church, ever arrive on the scene. The Latin phrase *missio Dei* (mission of God) was coined to emphasise that all mission is really God's mission and that we are called to join him in what he is already doing. Even Jesus said that he can do nothing by himself; only what he sees the Father doing (John 5:19).

This clarification of the dynamics of our missionary engagement with our world may sound subtle but it is important. It means that we cannot speak of the mission of the Church, as if it were some independent entity. David Bosch, a prominent author on the subject of mission, went on to describe mission as 'an attribute of God'. In other words, it is not just something he engages in, but it is an impulse grounded deep within the very heart of God; we could say that mission is who God is. This is an essential point. Although I have never been convinced that Latin is the best language in which to communicate to the Church today (my Catholic friends will have to forgive me), the term *missio Dei* emphasises God's prior activity and our need to partner with him. It is expressed in the well-known thought that 'it is not that the Church has a mission, but that the mission of God has a Church'. This emphasis can be attractive to those of us within the charismatic wing of the Church, as it alerts us to the need to hear the voice of the Spirit in mission. (The term mission refers to all aspects of those things Jesus did, as outlined in Luke 4:16-18. It includes announcing forgiveness, working for justice and being agents of healing).

An emphasis on the *missio Dei* has practical implications. When we believe that it is WE ourselves who have a mission then we tend to develop our own strategies to achieve God's goal on his behalf. This taps into our western belief in the power of the individual to achieve our aims through rationality and other human powers. We particularly rely on our ability to design goal-oriented strategies. When, on the other hand, we believe that God is *already* working in the world, *already* fulfilling *his* mission, our task is then to keep in step with the Spirit. This might, of course, involve some planning on our part, but then what is needed is more like a discernment process, where we seek to align ourselves with God and act *in response* to his will (see Acts 13:1-3).

From the record of the early Church outlined in the Acts of the Apostles, we can see that their approach resonates with the concept of the *missio Dei*. Generally speaking, it was God, rather than the apostles, who took the initiative in most situations. Acts 10 and 11 provides a great example of this dynamic - noting yet again that the starting point was availability in prayer. God had heard Cornelius's prayer and he also, with some considerable difficulty, sought to guide Peter as he prayed. Both

Cornelius and Peter experienced the presence of God in a vision (Acts 10:2-3 and 9). Peter was rather slow to understand what was going on, trying hard to keep up with the God who had already gone before him. He eventually realised that he should visit Cornelius but was astonished to find that God had already been working well beyond the bounds of the Church. To Peter's amazement, he got halfway through his talk when the Spirit took over. The account reads as if the Spirit is rather impatient, perhaps even bored by Peter's sermon, and doesn't wait for him to finish (Acts 10:44)! Even on the day of Pentecost, Peter was simply keeping up with God's action and he did not initiate anything himself. He just happened to be present and took the opportunity to explain the events unfolding before his eyes, starting with a disclaimer to drunkenness (Acts 2:15). As mentioned, that is not to overlook the fact that planning was involved in the account of the Church in Acts. We can see a certain logic in the route Paul took on his missionary journeys, but the emphasis on a 'missionary God' means that the apostles relied heavily on listening to those promptings of the Spirit. God often makes his presence known to people, despite our slowness to 'cotton on' to whatever he is doing. We play our part, but very much as junior partners who are trying to keep up.

This emphasis on partnering with God is good for our mental health. It saves us from feeling we have the overwhelming responsibility of carrying the weight of the world on our shoulders. It releases us to walk with the Lord, in the confidence that he has both gone before us and that we carry his presence with us. Our part is to be attentive and to look for signs of the Spirit's activity as we fulfil our call to have an impact on people and communities. Doing this by seeking to discern the presence and activity of the Spirit is a different approach to much of the early teaching which I imbibed as a young Christian, which seemed to put the onus on me. It sets us on a different course and shapes our approach to pilgrimage.

Embracing Vulnerable Situations

Pilgrimage involves risk. Walking with God sometimes means we have to 'walk on the water'. Like the disciples, as we set out from the security of the shore, we do not realise all that the journey will entail. I feel sorry for Peter, held up again and again in various stories, as an example of rashness. As he sought to reach his master despite the wind and the waves, he was a much better example of faith than many of his companions, who clung to the security provided by the boat. Peter was the only one who risked walking towards Jesus. 'Peters' are people who are more desperate to join Jesus than those of us who always weigh up the risk. We need to avoid recklessness, but when it's in response to having heard the voice of Jesus, faithfully stepping into a vulnerable situation often gets us closer to him. If we avoid the risk we keep our distance and become an observer of the life of faith, rather than an active participant.

Some of us, people who are probably very much like me, can identify more with Thomas in these sorts of situations. Following the death of Lazarus Jesus told the disciples of his intention to go to Judea, risking his life and putting the whole band of disciples in jeopardy. Thomas alone responds with a combination of resignation and faith 'let us go that we might die with him' (John 11:16). He was actually correct in his assessment as going to Judea enraged Jesus' opponents and they plotted against him. We might even say his assessment was prophetic, as tradition has it that Thomas was a martyr in India. In common parlance, we could say that he believed in the adage 'feel the fear and do it anyway'. Or perhaps, more insightfully, we might say that he was the first person willing to die for Jesus. I like this story of Thomas because it shows that pilgrimage is not just for optimists or the adventurous at heart, it is also for realists.

Pilgrimage, actively embracing vulnerable situations, involves a degree of anxiety, but oddly enough, doing so can free us from worry, because we then have no alternative but to rely on God. I am sometimes asked to speak to groups of people whom I find intimidating (either because they are clever, or more experienced, or more youthful, or because they look much more 'together' than I feel). I never engineer an invitation to speak somewhere so, in accepting an invitation, I have to remind myself that it was God who opened the door. As God created the opportunity the outcome is God's responsibility. The thought that the end result doesn't depend wholly on me enables me to relax. I sometimes find that the more vulnerable I feel, the more God seems to turn up on the day. Perhaps his power is made perfect in weakness, after all.

The Challenge

God's will is not always easy to embrace and it is often challenging. Pilgrimage requires us to have the single-mindedness of an athlete, determined to train hard and to perform well on the day. The temptation to relax or give up is a constant theme in the Bible. We see Abraham's family set out from Ur, under the leadership of Terah his father. The biblical record points out the fact that although they set out on their pilgrimage, they got waylaid (see Acts 7:3-4). Once they arrived in Haran they became settlers, no longer willing to be pioneers. Haran might have reminded them of their home in Ur, as the moon god was worshipped in both cities. It took a fresh call to get Abraham to resume the journey (Genesis 11:31-12:3). It is not always easy to continue our journey and we tend to seek the familiar rather than embrace the vulnerability that pilgrimage entails.

Jeremiah 12 recounts a story where the prophet is very fed up at finding himself in yet another vulnerable situation. He had already been through the mill and he had had enough. Sometimes people represent the Prophets of Israel as having unstable erratic personalities, but nothing could be further from the truth. Jeremiah is sometimes considered to have had a depressive personality. His complaining to God is seen as evidence of his being a 'glass-half-empty' person. But who would not complain when he found himself imprisoned and not feel peeved in such circumstances? God's initial call had seemed to imply that he would experience continual deliverance coupled with being given great authority in speaking to those in power (Jeremiah 1:8-10). In fact, the prophets of Israel needed to exhibit greater than average stability or they would not have survived their calling for any longer than a month or so, if that. They demonstrated exceptional perseverance in circumstances that must have created a huge sense of personal threat. Most of us would have looked for a way out of the call, as in the case of Jonah. God's response to Jeremiah's prayer of complaint might seem lacking in sympathy. Jeremiah is told to toughen up because he would find himself in even more vulnerable situations in the future: 'If you have raced men on foot, and they have wearied you, how will you compete with horses?' (Jeremiah 12:5). He was called to walk with God and embrace the journey, wherever his pilgrimage might lead, as indeed are we.

Paradoxically, this sort of (Celtic) pilgrimage is not a 'spiritual experience' as popularly conceived - we don't float across the landscape with a knowing, faith-filled smile, exuding a ring of confidence. We really *do* feel vulnerable and our faith is usually a mixture of active trust and insecurity. Our memory of the past, the story of how God turned up the last time we trusted him, can sometimes help, but a previous positive experience doesn't always make things easier the next time around, at least not for me. We need the stories of men and women of faith in the Bible to inspire us; we need to look to the example of Jesus, who looked to the joy set before him at the end of the journey (Hebrews 12:2). We also can draw inspiration from the example of the Celtic saints, men and women who achieved great things through their willingness to risk the journey of pilgrimage.

8

Possessions

A prominent characteristic of traditional monasticism is that of relinquishing possessions and money in order to pursue God's presence. This is a voluntary action, designed to facilitate freedom from attachment to material possessions, property or anything else which might act as a distraction to the main thing, which is knowing and following God.

Monks and nuns also renounce possessions to closely imitate Jesus, who seemingly owned very little. A vow of poverty was seen as a means of identification with Jesus and the Apostles. The father of monasticism, St Anthony, inherited great wealth but sold his possessions, and, after having made provision for his younger sister, gave the rest away to the poor. This pattern has been repeated innumerable times in the lives of Christian saints throughout the ages. Historically, St Anthony's example has been emulated by monastic orders as well as by Celtic saints.

St Aidan spent much time walking around the Northeast of England, evangelising and strengthening those who were already believers. Out of concern for the physical strain of so much walking, the king of the region gave him a horse for his travels. But the king had not reckoned on Aidan's generosity and the saint promptly gave the horse to the first poor person he met.

The significance of monastic poverty can however be overstated, as becoming part of a monastery community needs to be seen in historical context and could be said to have certain advantages. While monks have few personal possessions, they usually have access to communally owned resources including land, workshops and other amenities, in addition to which monasteries often provide a secure and stable environment for those who live there. The fact that in medieval times, monasteries owned farmland, orchards, livestock and stabling as well as many other buildings, in addition to churches and chapels within the monastery boundary, gave rise to much debate among Franciscans; as far as some were concerned, this constituted a form of joint ownership, incompatible with a life of poverty.

Following the Monastic Example

A few within New Monasticism have sought to emulate the monastic example of renouncing all but the basic necessities. Scott Bessenecker's book *The New Friars* tells the story of young people who, in the spirit of St Francis, have chosen to live among the poorest of the poor in the global South. While the majority of us do not embrace poverty for the sake of the Gospel in this way, we can recontextualise this aspect of monasticism in the form of generosity.

The Desert Fathers exhibited generosity towards strangers. They themselves would eat frugal 'peasant' meals while ensuring that any guests were provided for with sumptuous fare. Not realising that they were receiving special attention, being treated as Christ himself might be, sometimes such guests wrongly accused these early monks of living 'off the fat of the land', assuming that they too were eating extremely well. The same practice of reserving the best food for others characterised the monks at St David's monastery in Wales.

The subsequent history of monasticism includes other examples of restraint and self-denial and is epitomised by the vow of poverty taken by Franciscans. This involves giving up the right to possessing more than the minimum needed to survive and is done as an act of solidarity with the poor.

The sort of generosity we see in monasticism follows in the footsteps of Israel and the early Church. Generosity was enshrined in the Torah, where farmers had to leave the edges of their fields unharvested so that the poor could have access to some of the produce of the land (Leviticus 19:9-11).

Generosity also played a large part in the history of the Early Church: 'And they were selling their possessions and belongings and distributing the proceeds to all, as any had need' (Act 2:45). Their heightened awareness of the presence of God following Pentecost appears to have freed these early disciples from having to find security in their possessions. Acts 2 suggests that when the Spirit was powerfully active among early believers generosity happened spontaneously without being prompted. An unprecedented outpouring of generosity is a sign of - and the result of - the presence of the Spirit.

Generosity is a sign of the Spirit's presence, but it can also be a specific gift, given by the Spirit to some people who then excel in contributing to the material needs of others (Romans 12:8). Some people exude generosity, as in the case of Barnabas, who sold land and gave the proceeds to the apostles. Notice that he didn't stipulate how the apostles used the proceeds, something which can sometimes happen in the case of those who need to always be in control, but gave freely, laying the proceeds at the apostle's feet (Acts 4:36-37).

Generosity is a response to grace. It is the natural response to the realisation that God's gifts to us are wholly unmerited. The fact that we are recipients of God's generosity can also enable us to love ourselves more. After all, if God is so outrageously kind to us, if he welcomes us with open arms, perhaps it is true that we are loved extravagantly (Luke 15:20). Meditating on this fact, chewing it over, so that it sinks deeply into our very being, can help us be more kindly disposed towards ourselves, even at times when we have badly messed up. If, on the other hand, we find it hard to have a generous attitude towards *ourselves* we are likely to find it difficult to be generous to others.

Extravagant giving was a natural response for the woman who anointed Jesus' feet with oil; she 'wasted' her most expensive possession without a second thought, as she was overwhelmed with thankfulness (Luke 7:38). Grace leads to gratitude and Jesus could tell by her actions that this unnamed woman had already received the unmerited grace of God in forgiveness. But generosity is not just for those of us who have costly possessions. It is often the case that people who are materially poor are sometimes very generous with the little they do have, as Jesus observed in the case of a poor widow (Mark 12:41-44).

Financial Giving

One way to express generosity is to practise regular financial giving. A Rule can include the decision to give away a certain proportion of income to specific causes, to individuals or organisations. Having a Rule actually simplifies our lives, saving us from constantly having to make decisions about where and how much to give. Of course, regular giving as part of a Rule does not preclude additional giving to other causes.

It is good to choose areas of need which have meaning to us personally so that we can give wholeheartedly and happily, as authentic generosity only exists if we give willingly (2 Corinthians 9:7). We regularly give a small amount each month to a Catholic charity called Mary's Meals who do a truly amazing job feeding schoolchildren in the developing world. They started with a focus on 200 children in Malawi and now feed over one million each day. Without this food, many of these young people would need to work to feed themselves and would, therefore, be unable to attend school. I feel it is a privilege to be able to partner in a very small way with such a wonderful organisation.

Their aims have personal resonance for me, as I have myself stood in an African orphanage savouring (!) mealie meal broth, the regular lunch for the children. Mealie meal is a high energy food but bland in the extreme to someone from the West and I recall surreptitiously handing my mug of mealie meal to a child standing next to me; the child looked very pleased to be its recipient. Mary's Meals reminds me of this experience and how much a regular meal means to those in poverty. It has an emotional resonance for me and I feel tearful writing this. I have no difficulty believing that, particularly as far as mealie meal is concerned, it is more blessed to give than to receive and am aware that even a small act of giving can feel very rewarding.

Generosity can be a conscious decision and, although it is not always easy to part with our money or other resources, it can, in fact, have a very positive effect on our character. Henri Nouwen spoke of gratitude and generosity as being the antidotes to resentment. Personally though, I am unconvinced that actually *requiring* people to be generous is a good thing, which brings us to the topic of tithing.

Tithing

Tithing is a specific approach to financial giving. An in-depth look at the topic of *obligatory* tithing - giving a strict 10% of one's income to one's own church - is beyond the scope of this book, but here are a few brief comments:

Some Christians give 10% of their income to their church, regarding it as a scriptural directive, pointing out that it is mentioned in the Torah and that Jesus stated that he had not come to abolish the Law (Matthew 5:17-20). Many feel happy to continue this practice today and are able to contribute their tithe in a spirit of generosity. The drawback is that some people experience this as an external regulation and are then motivated by something other than generosity, such as guilt. Giving motivated by a sense of duty alone can make us feel resentful towards God.

An alternative approach to this strict form of tithing can also be argued from Scripture. This is the regular practice of generous giving with the individual determining the level of contribution to their church or elsewhere (see 2 Corinthians 8:8 in particular). This less prescriptive form of tithing balances the needs of the Church with other demands on the giver's income. I have friends on both sides of the tithing debate, some defending their view with feeling. I have never been personally convinced that a strict 10% tithe is required by Scripture and have belonged to two different churches where this form of tithing was taught. I was happy to go along with it and now regard it as being equivalent to a Rule of Life for those churches.

When we give to our local church we ourselves benefit from the facilities provided and the care we receive from a pastoral team. But other people definitely benefit from our giving, as non-members are drawn in and some other members who cannot afford to give much can enjoy the church's facilities. In addition, paid church staff may be involved in providing services such as preschool playgroups for the wider community and buildings may also be employed in this way. Whether we strictly tithe or have a looser approach, it is good to be as generous as possible towards those who lead churches and to ensure that their standard of living is in keeping with that of the local community.

Encouragement

Generosity extends to areas other than finance. It is very important to feel valued and we tend to thrive when others are generous in their praise and encouragement of us (as long as the praise is genuine). God's attitude towards us, one of generosity, restores our dignity and a similar dynamic operates when people encourage us or show in other ways that they respect and value us.

There is a story about Pope Francis which illustrates this, recounted by a woman who knew him when he was a cardinal in Argentina. She had become a sex worker to support her children and keep them out of poverty. He would walk past her each day on the street and always greeted her in a way that communicated great respect, something she might not have expected from a priest, as her profession was well known. His brief interaction with her, mostly in passing, gave her a sense of dignity. When we are treated with respect it has a positive impact on our sense of self-worth.

We can be generous in our attitude to others and seek to encourage, bless and build up one another. Barnabas is an example of this sort of generosity, as well as of financial generosity (Acts 4:36). His name means 'Son of Encouragement' and he has a significant role in the story of the Church as described in Acts. He offered personal support to Paul by extending to him the hand of friendship, at a time when others were very wary and avoided any contact. Barnabas later fell out with Paul over John Mark and demonstrated a more generous, perhaps a kinder, attitude to Mark than that of his more famous apostolic companion (who later seems to have had a change of heart and came around to valuing Mark once more).

Encouragement is vital but easy to neglect, and we can be alert for opportunities to be generous in spirit with our words. Speaking positively to someone, verbalising our appreciation of what they have done or who they are, comes naturally to some of us, but not to all. For those of us who are more reserved, the practice of encouraging others is a discipline with which we need to consciously engage. It is important as encouragement literally instils **courage** within us, enabling us to press on to greater things. Many of us, myself included, need the ministry of those who are generous with encouragement.

Generosity can be exercised through our regularly giving money to people or causes, and by giving encouragement, but we can also be generous in giving our time, as we employ our gifts on behalf of others.

Being Generous with our Time

Having gifts that differ according to the grace given to us, let us use them: if prophecy, in proportion to our faith; if service, in our serving; the one who teaches, in his teaching; the one who exhorts, in his exhortation; the one who contributes, in generosity; the leader, with zeal; the one who does acts of mercy, with cheerfulness.
ROMANS 12:6-7

In the list of gifts in Romans 12, Paul acknowledges that we have diverse gifts and encourages us to use the gifts we have been given - and, by implication, not to envy or seek to emulate the gift of others. We serve others best when we employ our unique talents, whether it is in providing emotional support, encouraging others or giving practical help. Although we should all be willing to help in whatever way is needed, we contribute best when we use the specific gifts we have been given. Perhaps as an aside, it is worth noting that Paul suggests leaders primarily serve by exercising their gift of leadership. They may be less gifted than others in, for example, acts of compassion or helping others practically and our expectations of the role of leadership need to be realistic.

I am very fortunate in being surrounded by generous people. In the lockdown of the Covid-19 pandemic, our church had to develop the ability to use social networking platforms. One very generous person spent an enormous amount of time ensuring that even the most tech-phobic person has had good access to Zoom. This may not have been in his mind when Paul wrote his letter to the Romans, but it is an example of the gift of compassion/acts of mercy (Romans 12:7). Without being able to effectively use Zoom many people would have felt extremely isolated and disconnected from their church family.

This chapter has attempted to explore how we might consider the monastic example of embracing voluntary poverty, as a means to be free from our attachment to things. It has been suggested that our developing practices of generosity is one way to recontextualise the monastic vow of poverty. Regarding ourselves as stewards is a way of freeing ourselves from the hold possessions can have over us. Generosity can improve our spiritual health. The rich, young ruler needed to give away all that he owned, not as a symbolic act to prove himself to be a radical disciple, but to save him from trusting wholly in his possessions (Luke 18:18-22). Practising generosity is a means of escaping from the delusion that money and material things are our main source of security (1 Corinthians 10:13). Generosity frees us to actively trust God and in doing so we are more likely to know his provision and experience his presence in our lives.

9

Pride

Prior to the eleventh century, the church considered the chief vice to
be pride...
GREG PETERS (THE STORY OF MONASTICISM)

There is a connection between possessions and pride, which was clearly
recognised by, among many others, St Basil the Great (329-379AD), the
father of Eastern Monasticism. In his early days as an orator, Basil
enjoyed great success as a highly sought-after speaker and was tempted
severely by pride. He became fearful that this pride would overtake his
piety, and as a result, sold all that he had, giving away the proceeds and
becoming a priest and monk. Pride is a besetting sin whenever things go
well for us, or when we feel we have achieved something noteworthy.
We naturally want others to acknowledge us and love us, but pride
demands that we are admired. It is listed as a cardinal ('deadly') sin by
all branches of the Church, often portrayed as being the foundation for
all other sins. Isaiah 14 and Ezekiel 28 describe the pride of two near
eastern kings, but these passages are often interpreted as referring to a
more cosmic event which resulted from pride, that of Satan's fall.

Humility is the opposite to pride and it is the quality we most need in
order to walk with God (Micah 3:8). Humility cultivates God's presence,
whereas pride alienates him since God is opposed to the proud. Of the
two options, and there are only two, humility is clearly better as it is
based on the reality that we have humble origins, created from the dust
of the earth. Pride, on the other hand, is founded on self-deception, the

grandiose delusion that we are special and gifted, perhaps even exceptional. God allowed the Apostle Paul to be severely afflicted to prevent pride from creeping in (2 Corinthians 12:7). Particularly pernicious is so-called spiritual pride, a tendency which was continually countered by Jesus in his interaction with the Pharisees.

Celtic monks and nuns took the danger of pride very seriously and sought to overcome it by taking a vow of obedience. Ian Bradley, in *Colonies of Heaven,* notes that they 'lived according to some kind of disciplinary code and accepted the authority of the abbot'. Discipline was very strict by modern standards and even minor infringements would result in harsh punishment, designed to help the miscreant reform. There was a strong puritanical strain in Celtic monasticism with an emphasis on denying the will, as Bradley points out in *Following the Celtic Way.*

Certainly, the wider cultural setting shaped the way in which the vow of obedience was outworked by the Celtic Church. The expectation of obedience to 'superiors' reflected the hierarchical nature of a society founded on the existence of a local ruling elite, consisting of kings and princes. Although the Celtic Church is sometimes portrayed as being a non-hierarchical egalitarian ideal, freer and less rule-bound than the 'Church of Rome', this is pure myth.

Despite what we may consider its extremes, any monastic inspired spirituality needs to consider the significance of obedience. Today we emphasise the desirability of so-called 'flat', non-hierarchical, structures and the discipline of obedience is something we can easily discard as belonging to an earlier, less enlightened age. But an awareness of the thinking behind the monastic vow of obedience, taken as the antidote to pride, might help us to reframe this practice.

Obedience

The concept of obedience is central to a monastic Rule as it creates order by establishing respect for those who exercise authority within the monastery. Benedict's Rule also values mutual submission, recognising that each of us can contribute our insights, alongside the wisdom provided by our 'superiors' (Ephesians 5:21). Sociological factors are also involved - monasteries are complex social organisations with common aims and clear goals which require an appropriate organisational structure. As with any such group, hierarchies exist in order to ensure that they keep on track with their avowed purpose and mission.

It is important to recognise that becoming a monk is a voluntary act, with obedience as an accepted part of the package. Those who join monastic orders make a conscious decision to conform to the particular Rule of that monastery and to follow the practical decisions made by its leadership (who are themselves bound by that Rule). Such formal leadership structures are necessary - without them, there is often a power struggle, sometimes hidden beneath the surface, and the most dominant people usually control the decisions of the group.

Spiritual leadership is expected of an abbot or abbess. Churches, monasteries and religious organisations can certainly glean insights from the world of business, but the central issue for spiritual leadership is beyond the scope of any secular model. Exodus 33:14-16 hints that the main skill which is required for leadership is discerning when we are moving with God's presence and in God's Spirit - and when we are simply just moving. It is not just a case of being good at planning, skilled in organisational development or having the personal charisma which others naturally follow. This perspective is in keeping with the New Testament where leadership is regarded primarily as a gift from God (Romans 12:8).

The goal of spiritual leadership is to form individuals and communities in the way of Christ (Ephesians 4:11-13). Although some leaders are entrepreneurial, spiritual leadership is not to be confused with being a religious entrepreneur. The main image of leadership employed throughout the Bible is that of the caring shepherd, leading a flock to find suitable pasture and fresh water. A godly abbot or abbess will be primarily concerned with the growth and welfare of those who are led.

A further contrast with secular models of leadership is found in 1 Corinthians 12:28 where Paul uses a term related to navigation. Derek Tidball, in *Builders and Fools*, points out that spiritual leadership is the God-given ability to pilot a church, or other religious entity, so that there is movement together in the right direction. Although planning and the principles of change management are helpful, church leadership is first and foremost a matter of discernment and of being led by the Spirit.

Keeping this in mind can help us as we consider the place of monastic obedience today.

Reframing Obedience

Good leadership creates security by providing healthy boundaries. In recent years theorists have recognised that the other side of leadership is followership. This refers to the way in which people in organisations respond to leadership and it relates to the more ancient concept of obedience. Our expectations as followers are partly determined by our cultural background. More directive approaches to leadership are often encountered in countries where society as a whole is less egalitarian and we expect more consultative approaches in the West.

We can be wary of terms such as obedience, because of the potential for domineering or controlling leadership to emerge. We are also aware that even where more egalitarian leadership structures are seen as the ideal, abuse and bullying still occur, even despite safeguards being in place (and we should also note that leaders can themselves be bullied by people in their church congregations or communities).

The particular shape that obedience has taken in the Church over the centuries, including in more recent times, is less than encouraging. We are aware that in seeking to create leadership structures we can, as one prominent theologian has put it, create 'domination structures'. Certain features to do with the practice of obedience expected in the Celtic Church also give cause for concern, which means that we need to adapt rather than adopt their approach. It is tempting to shelve the issue altogether, but to do so is to throw out the baby with the bathwater since obedience is actually a biblical concept.

Despite these legitimate concerns, Ian Adams argues in *Cave, Refectory, Road* that we have much to learn from the example of monastic obedience. He points out that monastic movements prioritise the common good and focus on what would most benefit the whole community. This emphasis is somewhat different from that of our own settings, where the needs and wants of individuals are considered to be of greater importance than those of the community. While we might regard a community as existing to serve the individual, Adams suggests that the discipline of obedience encourages 'each monk not to place themselves in the centre of any decision'. It is not that individuals are regarded as being unimportant, but we might consider whether the pendulum has swung too far in the direction of the primacy of the individual, emphasising *my* needs and *my* wants. Focusing on ourselves is unlikely to cultivate God's presence.

Ian Adams links monastic obedience to humility. We often regard ourselves as the most important person in the room, which is a form of socially sanctioned narcissism. Such a misguided view needs urgent attention - for the good of those around us, as well as for our own good. We can elevate our own opinions above those of others, a form of pride, reminiscent of the last verse in the book of Judges where we read that 'Everyone did what was right in their own eyes' (21:25). Today we might rephrase this as 'everyone does what is right according to their own personal truth'. The monastic emphasis on obedience is not simply a reflection of their cultural setting but has deep theological roots.

Humility in Action

The original monks and nuns in the Egyptian desert emphasised the importance of humility. John of the Thebaid wrote:

Above all, a monk should be humble. For this is the Saviour's first commandment, 'Blessed are the poor in spirit, for theirs is the kingdom of heaven'.

These early monastics regarded obedience as the means by which they undertook a lifelong training in humility, freeing them from the tyranny of any narcissistic view of themselves. Syncletica, one of the Desert Mothers, expressed this view clearly:

It seems to me that for those who live in monasteries obedience is a higher virtue than chastity, however perfect. Chastity is in danger of pride; obedience has the promise of humility.

Similarly, Benedict regarded humility as a means of taming the insistence that *my* will be done. It is important that we learn to differentiate our own will from God's will - they occasionally concur, but probably less often than we might believe. This is made explicit in the following extracts from Benedict's Rule (7:31 & 34):

> The second step of humility is not to delight in satisfying our desires out of a love for our own way.
> The third step of humility is to submit to the superior in all obedience for love of God.

Before looking at how we might re-appropriate monastic obedience for today, it is worth considering what the Bible has to say about humility, stretching back to Creation itself.

Dust

Human, humus (earth or dust) and *humility* are terms which come from the same root. Human beings were created from the elements of the earth, a curious mixture of dust and the breath of God (Genesis 2:7). Humility is the acceptance that we have these lowly origins and we are, therefore, limited beings. This has a very positive effect on our inner world, as it enables us to make peace with our limitations, as well as allowing us to celebrate our strengths. Humility frees us from having overly high expectations of ourselves and of others in a world that often demands impossible standards. We *can* escape this toxic situation, which always leaves us feeling that we are failures (not just that we have failed but that we, in ourselves, are failures). Humility is being comfortable in our own skin, so comfortable that we don't feel the need to justify ourselves to others or to bolster our reputation.

The ultimate act of humility was seen when Jesus trusted the Father so completely that he became a vulnerable human baby and later submitted to death on a cross. His willingness to humble himself had a paradoxical outcome: he refused to elevate himself and, as a result of his refusal, he was raised to the right hand of God. God the Father exalted Jesus *because* he refused to exalt himself and the same dynamic works in our lives as well (Philippians 2:8-9; 1 Peter 5:6).

Humility is relying on God, rather than on ourselves, in the sure knowledge that he gives the grace (the ability to succeed) to the humble (James 4:6). When we see God act, it increases our sense of security and makes us aware of His presence with us. We become aware that the One acting on our behalf is giving us the very thing which we have been unable to grasp for ourselves. It is the meek (humble) who will inherit the land, rather than those whose hope is based on power, rights, skills or privilege. (Notice that Matthew 5:5 reiterates Psalm 37:11, which is worth reading to gain insight into the point Jesus was making). To act meekly, trusting God alone, is profoundly counter-cultural and very different from seeking to reach our 'full potential' as independent autonomous entities. Pride engenders self-reliance; humility frees us from total dependence on our own insights and abilities.

Humility & Mental Health

Humility is sometimes portrayed as involving the adoption of a negative view of ourselves, but in fact, humility releases us to be who we really are, without the need for pretence. It engenders self-acceptance and saves us from having to construct a *false self* to convince ourselves and others that we are worthy of acceptance, love and admiration. Our *true self* is potentially less impressive than we would like to be but is more peaceful, less self-absorbed and easier to be with.

Thomas Merton puts the heart of the matter quite succinctly: 'In order to become myself I must cease to be what I always thought I wanted to be'. We do not need to aspire to be more gifted, good looking, athletic or intelligent than we already are. Humility is a great blessing, as it frees us from the need to be defensive about our shortcomings. It releases us from our desire to dominate others so that we feel superior; we don't have to impress friends and colleagues to get the recognition we crave.

The British psychoanalyst Donald Winnicott was the first person to point out the existence of this true self/false self dichotomy - an internal struggle which causes much suffering to ourselves and those around us. Humility is the recognition of the fact not only that we are created from dust, but also that we are created in the image of God and endowed with great dignity. Keeping both these things in mind is good for our mental health, as well as for our spiritual wellbeing. Recognising that we are limited in terms of knowledge and competence, frees us from the paralysis we experience when we feel we must at all costs make the 'right' decision. We are unlikely to make perfect decisions every time as living systems are far too complex for certainty; something weather forecasters know only too well. Parents and politicians, our children, church leaders and employers are also 'humus' and will inevitably get it wrong as well much of the time - their most important quality, like ours, needs to be humility.

Humility, accepting our limitations, enables God to work through us more effectively and it puts us in good company. The Gospels, Mark's in particular, intentionally highlight the way the disciples always seemed to get hold of the wrong end of the stick, often compounding their incompetence by suggesting a foolish course of action. When Jesus speaks metaphorically they take it literally and vice versa. The good news is that if God could use them so powerfully, despite their obvious limitations, then he can use us as well. His power really is made perfect in our weakness (2 Corinthians 12:9).

Monastic Obedience

Humility enables us to benefit from the wisdom of others, but monastic obedience implies more than simply considering good advice. The centrality of obedience in the Celtic Church is evident when we consider the life of one of its most famous saints, Columba. It is difficult to be certain about the factors which led Columba to found his monastery on Iona, but one account suggests that whilst in an Irish abbey, he had illegally copied a manuscript - a form of intellectual theft. His refusal to apologise for his actions resulted in a war in which many were killed; as a result, he was banished from his homeland, a penance imposed by Church authorities. Whether this is historically accurate or not, and scholars disagree, it does illustrate the degree to which stern discipline *could* be imposed upon a monk.

We are unlikely to tolerate such stern disciplinary measures today, but this story might lead us to consider the extent to which we are accountable to others for our actions. In the New Testament, Paul's apostolic team is seen to have had a clear structure with a leadership hierarchy in place and could be cited as a biblical example of obedience in operation. Paul's authority was exercised in the way he directed his associates, sometimes sending them to specific cities or asking that specific people be sent to him.

How does this translate to our context? Obedience to a Rule and submission to an abbot or abbess is not as foreign to today's church as we might at first think. If, for instance, someone joins a mission organisation or works for a Bible College then that person is signing up to the values or doctrinal statement of that college or organisation (in effect, its Rule). This has some resonance with the decision taken by a monk or nun to enter a monastery or convent. Joining a Christian organisation today involves a commitment to respect the decisions of the trustees and CEO, even when those decisions might directly affect that person's role in the organisation. In a local church, we would not expect the same degree of 'obedience' that we might encounter in a monastery (or in a Christian organisation), but members are still expected to abide by certain ground rules. These might include a respect for the teaching of the New Testament and for their church's constitution or tradition.

These are examples where the concept of monastic obedience correlates with what might occur today but there is also a more general principle in operation. This involves the degree to which we consider ourselves to be accountable - answerable - to others and is an important issue, especially in churches which stress freedom and being led by the Spirit. Some people suggest that we are answerable only to God, but Scripture puts a high value on submission to one another and mutual *inter*dependence (Ephesians 5:21). Christians disagree as to what this means in practice but it counters our tendency to become 'a law unto ourselves'. The least it means is that we consider seriously what others say to us, particularly when the others in question have lives which embody the Gospel.

Listening to Others

Obedience, a prominent feature of Celtic monasticism, is actually a biblical concept, not simply a reflection of a particular cultural setting.

Scripture employs the terms 'obey' and 'submit', but not in a way which implies that we should obey others indiscriminately or follow advice which violates our conscience; definitely not in the sense of blind obedience. The Greek word used in the New Testament for obey is *hupakouo,* which literally is translated as 'listen under'. We are encouraged to be attentive to other people and to be open to persuasion.

The writer to the Hebrews encouraged his readers to obey their leaders but the context of his letter is all-important (13:17). He was writing to Christians in Rome who were experiencing persecution. Verse 7 of the same chapter indicates that the leaders in question were exemplary Christians, whose faith under pressure was worthy of imitation. 'Obedience' was an exhortation to conform to the example and teaching of leaders of the suffering church; leaders who were living demonstrations of what it meant to be faithful followers of Jesus.

This is not the exercise of personal power by one person over another, and in acknowledging that, we might have reservations about St Francis' attitude to monastic obedience: 'Inferiors should sacrifice their wills to God, and act as the superior wishes, even when they think certain things are better or more useful to their souls than what the superior commands'. We are aware we have blind spots and that others sometimes see what might be best for us, but we tend to be more comfortable with the thought that persuasion is preferable to command.

It is worth noting that the monastic Rule requiring obedience and submission is designed to be conducive to discipleship, and that for us, the main issue is whether we are open to persuasion; whether we seriously consider what others have to say to us. There is no warrant in Scripture whatsoever for churches to engage in 'heavy shepherding' where people's decisions about finances, careers and so on are controlled.

Benedict's Rule emphasises interdependence, our need for one another. He was quite scathing about certain independent monks whom he termed 'gyrovagues' (meaning 'aimless wanderers' in Latin). These were self-styled people who refused to submit to the authority of an abbot or abbess. They fashioned their own personally-crafted Rule, designed to allow them to do whatever they fancied. There are many Christians today, including some prominent leaders, who fit this description, effectively independent, not part of any church, organisation or a wider forum where they might frequently be exposed to the wisdom of others. We are inventive creatures who can find many ways to evade the healthy restrictions implied by 'listen under'.

On the other hand, Benedict realised that the concept of obedience can be applied in ways which contravene a monk's autonomy. His Rule guards against this possibility by ensuring that decision making is done in a consultative manner. If a monk is assigned a task which he feels is inappropriate there is room for appeal, although the abbot's decision is final. This may seem harsh, but as previously stated, it reflects the sense that monks are part of a body and need to do what is deemed necessary for the overall wellbeing of the whole community. It is clearly a complex issue as we seek a path between individualism, everyone doing 'what is right in their own eyes', and authoritarianism, where a leader or the group controls individuals.

Humility & Accountability

Humility is important in a world where our strongly held views, hunches and feelings get confused with objective truth. Our feelings may well contain an aspect of the truth, revelation even, but they need careful assessment. It is easy to be blinded by the light of our own revelation and we benefit from dialogue, particularly when our decisions affect others. Regularly seeking the opinions of those who are more experienced or wiser than we are, should be not be considered an optional extra.

When we seek contexts for accountability we pursue humility, the heart of monastic obedience. Arguably, we in the West have gone overboard on the idea of accountability with a tendency to create highly bureaucratic systems, which are often ineffective and so risk-averse that they stifle adventure and innovation. Nonetheless, accountability is vital partly because we tend to gradually develop bad practices, or sinful habits even, little by little, often imperceptibly.

A lack of a desire for accountability can be a symptom of pride, but past experiences where accountability has been abused can also make us wary. Even so, humility will always lead us back to a place of listening carefully to others. Deep listening is an aspect of meaningful friendships, especially where there are no holds barred in terms of what can be discussed. We might also explore our decisions or actions with close family members, a spiritual director, a counsellor or a mentor. The Celtic practice of having a soul friend, *Anam Cara* in Gaelic, is another way to be open and accountable. Soul friends are people with whom we can talk freely about our inner world and they provide the benefit of their observations or advice.

More formal contexts, such as an accountability group or a board, are vital for those of us who hold formal positions of leadership. Such structures can, however, be subverted and those who are self-assured sometimes ignore accountability structures when the advice given is unpalatable. Because of this, for us to have a genuine appreciation of the wisdom of accountability is more fundamental than the shape or form of any accountability structure. We need to realise our propensity for self-deception. We often cling on to any blind spots as if they are old friends! Others can see what we cannot and humility recognises that we ourselves are not the font of all wisdom, either for our own lives or for those of others.

In order to create effective accountability structures, we need to involve people on a peer level who respect us but who realise that we are as frail and limited as any other human being. Sometimes gifted leaders create 'pseudo-accountability' structures by surrounding themselves with easily persuadable people. Accountability structures which consist of people who place the leader on a pedestal never work - being asked to join one by a respected church leader may be flattering, but as such, is set to fail.

Openness

When we are habitually open with others it creates a depth of relationship. When we stick with surface issues it creates superficial friendships which can lead to boredom and disconnection, rather than to fostering genuine friendship. Genuine humility, rather than alienating others as pride does, creates lasting connections between people. I have a friend, a Christian leader, who decided to admit to others (in other words 'to confess') that he felt quite vulnerable. He decided to respond when he's asked, 'How are you?' by freely admitting that he was suffering from anxiety. This could have resulted in people thinking of him as being weak and unfit to lead. Instead, he found that his honesty had an unexpected effect: in response, some very together-looking people began to open up about their own personal struggles. Rather than decreasing his social standing, being vulnerable allowed the possibility of shared experience. In other words, humility creates community. Rather than being a sign of weakness, being humble requires a certain strength. Humility takes much more courage than pretending that we are something we are not.

There have been people in my own life with whom I have been able to reach a real level of honesty. Such relationships have nearly always had a very positive outcome. The common element has been actively embracing the opportunity presented to be open about my struggles, conflicts and shortcomings. Openness is not easy for an Englishman with a certain sort of upbringing and there can be a sense of shame when we express our lived reality, when we say, 'this is me'.

Shame as a Barrier to Accountability

Shame is experienced by most people, the exception being those with psychopathic or sociopathic personality disorders, who lack remorse or shame. Shame is highlighted in the biblical story of Adam and Eve, who were originally *'naked but not ashamed'* (Genesis 2:25). As a result of sin, they became aware of their vulnerable condition (3:7). Their eyes were opened to their nakedness and the result was that Adam hid from the presence of God. He could not bear the thought of being seen for who he really was, which is the essence of shame (3:10). Notice that sin was not the cause of his nakedness, but it created the sense that he was innately unacceptable, constitutionally inadequate. Of course, there is a sense in which we are not good enough due to sin, but the shame we are considering is different - it is the sense that I, the person God created in his image, is innately unworthy of love. Shame alienates us from God and each other and it disables us, so we hide from rather than cultivate God's presence.

Guilt and shame are different. Shame relates to who we are, guilt relates to what we have done, said or thought. *Guilt* is a term derived from the Anglo-Saxon word for gold, *geld* - guilt can be paid for, atoned for with gold or its equivalent. When we do things wrong our guilt is often accompanied by a legitimate sense of shame ('I feel bad that I have done such a thing'), but the shame we can experience day by day often relates to *who we are,* rather than particular wrong actions. We feel there is a flaw, a basic fault deep within us and, like Adam, we take action to hide our sense of shame - in our case we might construct the false self we mentioned earlier, to hide from others, ourselves and God. This can make us feel more legitimate, but it alienates us from others, as we have become inauthentic.

Confession

Humility involves our being honest about our shortcomings and the idea of confessing our sins to others is quite biblical (James 5:16). There is a sense in which this was no big deal for many of the Celtic saints, as penitence was seen as a normal component of their spirituality. St Patrick's autobiography begins with the words: 'My name is Patrick. I am a sinner, a simple country person, and the least of all believers'. This reads like someone introducing themselves at an Alcoholics Anonymous meeting (akin to 'my name is Patrick and I am an alcoholic'). It is just the way things are - human/humus, a sinner.

Catholic friends tell me that they experience great benefit from confessing their sins to a priest. They are in no doubt that it is God who forgives, but they report that confession helps break the power of sin, as well as reinforcing the fact that they are indeed forgiven. Paradoxically, admitting our faults and weaknesses to others can be a freeing experience. Once we tell another person about a particular sin or an area of weakness, it no longer exerts the hold that a powerful secret can have over us.

'Confession' is a concept that encompasses more than bringing our sins into the open. We can follow Paul's example and be honest about our struggles as well. The same Paul who elsewhere (helpfully) writes that we should bring our anxieties to God and leave them at his feet, told a whole church that he experienced 'anxiety for all the churches' as a daily burden for him to bear (Philippians 4:6-7 compared with 2 Corinthians 11:28). He confessed to being anxious each day; this is different from those who suggest we should have a sort of Zen-like detachment when anxiety creeps upon us. Developing a sense of detachment from suffering and affliction is a major goal of Buddhism, but not of Christianity.

Leadership & Accountability

It has been suggested that monastic obedience relates to the modern concept of accountability. It has also been suggested that different degrees of authority and different sorts of obedience are appropriate in different contexts. Clearly, a monastery requires a different approach to that of a local church, but whatever the setting we need to guard our attitude towards those who have executive authority in, for instance, Christian organisations or residential communities.

No structure for accountability is perfect but some are 'good enough'. Despite this, most systems can be subverted and we hear of several prominent leaders who have found ways to ignore accountability structures, and who when called to account, simply leave and go elsewhere. Sadly they lack a spirit of accountability, something which is more important than having the 'right' structure. The fact that they can often easily find another context for ministry is a symptom of greater value being placed on gift than on character. This is a reversal of biblical priorities and Jesus explicitly speaks out against gifted prophets and healers who are *lawless*, which is his term for being unaccountable (Matthew 7:22).

Using structures for accountability and practising humility and openness are ways to re-contextualise the monastic practice of obedience. The alternative to humility is pride, which, according to Ian Bradley, was considered by the Celtic Church to be 'the most deadly of sins' (*Following the Celtic Way*).

Pride is a particular temptation for Christian leaders who rise to prominence. Far too many, although starting well, succumb to pride once they receive acclamation. Of course, this is understandable as God often uses years of hardship or obscurity to prepare us for 'success' and once we achieve something we can come to feed on applause. These words of Thomas a Becket to a close friend on becoming archbishop of Canterbury in 1154 are pertinent:

Hereafter, I want you to tell me, candidly and in secret, what people are saying about me. And if you see anything in me that you regard as a fault, feel free to tell me in private. For from now on, people will talk about me, but not to me. It is dangerous for men of power if no one dares tell them when they go wrong.

10

People

Cultivating God's presence is not something we do for our own benefit alone. It is also for the benefit of other people - our friends, family and the wider community. God's presence is communicated, or carried, as we relate to others.

Hospitality and *proximity* are the two concepts that sum up ways in which Celtic Christians sought to relate to other people. I have found these two terms very helpful in considering how we should approach others - and how these concepts inform a Rule of Life. Hospitality and proximity are linked, but we will look at them in turn, with a chapter given to each. Assuming that God's presence is being cultivated in our lives, hospitality and proximity are the means by which God's presence can be carried with us so that the lives of those around us might also be affected. This chapter focuses on hospitality and the next on proximity.

When we hear the word 'hospitality' we often think of providing food, but for many of us, it can be daunting if we have to prepare a beautifully presented meal - perhaps we are not good cooks, or we feel anxious at the prospect of having guests in our home. We shy away from the idea of hospitality if we believe we need somehow to compete with MasterChef, as well as create a conducive atmosphere with gentle background music and dimmed lighting, accompanied with good wines. Besides which, many of us are not natural dinner-party conversationalists. Perhaps a more constructive view of hospitality is to see it as intentionally making space for others.

The heart of hospitality is being welcoming and attentive to other people. This can, in itself, be something we may need to learn, but thought of in this way, hospitality can demonstrate God's attitude towards others through the quality of our presence with them. I know of one senior Christian leader, who as a young man from a secular background, was welcomed warmly by Christians into their home. Their hospitality towards him not only made a deep impression on him but actually opened up the start of his Christian journey.

Creating Space for Others

Monasteries developed in the so-called Dark & Middle Ages and many offered shelter to travellers. By seeking to meet the needs of strangers they believed they were offering hospitality to Jesus himself (Matthew 25:40). This view reframes our simple acts of kindness, giving them great dignity. It transforms the value we put on performing menial, ordinary actions and it alerts us to the presence of God in *others*, particularly his presence with us in the shape of those in need.

By providing accommodation for visitors to stay overnight, monasteries became forerunners of the Holiday Inn, but with no bill to settle. The building where guests slept was called the *hospitium,* the Latin word from which we get the term 'hospitality'. Over time some monasteries also included an infirmary to care for the sick, which is how we in the West developed *hospitals.* They literally made space for others - a physical space in this case - which was not necessarily an easy task in the middle of their already busy lives.

There is a Rabbinic story which encapsulates the heart of hospitality: when God wanted to create the universe he realised that he already filled everything, so he had to make some space in which his new creation could exist. Because he was present everywhere he had to withdraw from somewhere to allow the physical world to have its own space. I like that story because hospitality, making the other person the centre of our attention, can only happen when we ourselves withdraw and make space - either literally giving the time to others, or metaphorically by focusing on another person, removing ourselves from the centre of attention.

Hospitality Brings its Own Rewards

Hospitality involves our welcoming and attending to the other. Most of us, even from a very early age, are naturally hospitable: children spontaneously chat with other children, making contact quite unselfconsciously. The desire to be hospitable carries its own reward in terms of friendship, even though, at times, it may be rejected. Whether our offer of hospitality is accepted or not, we are still cultivating God's presence: Jesus liked a hospitable atmosphere and he is still attracted to the company of hospitable people. Hospitality should come to characterise our churches and our lives.

Hospitality cannot be formulaic and it doesn't work if we try to imitate other people's gifts - the important thing is that we welcome others in whatever way comes naturally to us. This will often be rewarding for us because we have a sense of fulfilment whenever we use our God-given gifts. Hospitality is best done when it expresses the genuine desire to serve others in our own unique way. It is less attractive when it is done as a dutiful exercise in self-sacrifice. Once we discover our natural hospitality niche we experience for ourselves that it genuinely is more blessed to give than to receive (Acts 20:35). We can, of course, put on an act of being hospitable, simply to prove to ourselves we are good people, but genuine hospitality will always focus on the other person, not on the part we ourselves play.

Practising hospitality can have a further beneficial side effect: it enables us to become better people, despite our all too obvious imperfections. Acting hospitably can increase our sense of self-worth, as we often find we like *ourselves* better when we act hospitably. Furthermore, hospitality takes us beyond any tendency to introspection, since making someone else the centre of our attention helps us be less obsessed with ourselves. As we move away from self-absorption, the more likeable we become to other people and, again, their response to us will have a beneficial effect on our sense of self-esteem. Hospitality creates this virtuous circle.

The writer to the Hebrews encouraged us to be hospitable to strangers, holding out the tantalising possibility that we might be entertaining angels though being unaware of the fact (Hebrews 13:2). This injunction is in keeping with a long tradition among Semitic peoples, who count it a duty to provide hospitality to passers-by. A friend recounted that during his travels in the Saudi desert he was given a meal by nomadic peoples whom he had never met before. The fact that we might, unknowingly, be entertaining a messenger of God suggests we might miss out on all that God has for us if we neglect hospitality. What is more, hospitality is a way of imitating God, as hospitality is the heart of the Gospel.

The Gospel

Once we were outsiders, but God shows his love towards us by inviting us into his inner circle; an act of pure hospitality. The parable of the prodigal son continues to be one of the most well-known stories told by Jesus. It demonstrates that motivated by (undeserved) kindness, the Father is truly hospitable, welcoming us into his presence with outstretched arms, even despite our bad choices (Luke 15:20). He has made it possible for us to become part of his family and continues to include us, forgiving our faults, often on a daily basis.

Having freely received such unmerited kindness our response is to express that same kind welcome to others so that hospitality is a way in which our gratitude naturally finds an outlet. In this way, our experience of God's grace gets passed on to others. We see a similar dynamic in our everyday encounters: if when driving, someone lets you out of a side road you are then yourself more inclined to do the same for other drivers. How much greater than this is the debt of love we owe to the Father? Hospitality is the natural outflow of our having experienced the Gospel. Grace causes us to be gracious. Once we begin to view situations or decisions through the lens of hospitality we become aware that it is everywhere in the Bible. It pervades the Scriptures and if we keep the word *hospitality* in mind when reading the Bible we become aware that different facets of hospitality are encapsulated in a variety of biblical stories and teachings.

The Gospel involves God love for the whole world, but it is also very personal, as God loves each of us as unique individuals. Genuine hospitality can only be experienced when we recognise the uniqueness of the person before us. For hospitality to be experienced as genuinely positive the recipient needs to feel that we see them for who they really are and that we appreciate the nature of their needs. As a unique individual, the other person is different from you and me and unlikely to respond or think as we might. This sounds obvious, but it is very easy to project onto others what we think we would want in their situation or to fit them into a category so that we think we know best how to approach them.

I was involved in psychotherapy and counselling for many years, including as a supervisor and trainer. Through my experiences of that time, I discovered difficulties with approaches to counselling which seek to fit the experience of others into pre-existing theoretical frameworks. Although there are patterns in human experience, too much reliance on our pre-existing ideas leads to individual people being seen merely as particular examples of universal experiences of grief, abuse or neglect. The result is dehumanising, as such approaches fail to regard people as being unique and individual. Similarly in everyday life, we can be prone to thinking that we really know either what other people are like or what they are or should be saying - we can even finish off their sentences for them (which almost invariably means we are deaf to what they actually want to say). People usually realise when they are being objectified and will stop trying to communicate anything meaningful to us. One famous psychoanalyst suggested that the therapist should begin every session 'without memory or desire'. What he meant, was not to rely on what we think we already know about someone (memory) and to avoid trying to steer someone to the end we desire for them (desire). I think there is something in that approach that we can learn from in our everyday encounters with others.

Finding a Good Fit

It is also important to know ourselves well, including our gifts, abilities, and limitations. There are likely to be certain contexts in which each of us is more at ease and, therefore, naturally more hospitable. Some of us are much better when we set definite time aside for others; others of us feel more comfortable being spontaneous. It is good to realise that we are not all the same. We can choose to avoid comparing ourselves with others and concentrate on the strengths which God has given us.

111

Each of us has a different capacity for hospitality and we need to factor that into account so that we learn how best to be hospitable with our particular personality. If we are extroverted we will find ourselves energised by people contact, but not so introverts, who do best when they are hospitable more intermittently, with periods alone to recharge their batteries. Introverts can be very sociable but usually in short bursts.

Finding a good fit between our personalities, strengths, weaknesses and the particular people with whom we have contact is important. My experience would suggest that God sometimes gives grace to us to enable us to help more challenging people - and that sometimes he doesn't. Knowing the difference can help us discern where to focus our efforts. Engaging with a Rule includes our finding practices which help us to be hospitable to others, taking these personal factors into account.

Interruptibility

One example of how hospitality can be expressed in daily life involves the concept of '*interruptibility*'. This simply means being willing to allow others to interrupt us and this can be quite a challenge (except when filling in annual tax returns, when any interruption is welcomed). This particular practice does not come naturally to me, as usually, I want to plough on with whatever task is in hand and finish what I have started. If we are very task-orientated we may need to timetable some fallow time into our day, so that we have some built-in capacity to be interrupted without tasks simply backing up.

Hospitality is about making people feel valued and when we meet them in the street or at work, we allow them to 'fill the space'. This means we have to decide beforehand that we will focus on their interests and do more listening than talking, which is hard work for those of us with more expressive personalities. Active listening is involved and this requires us to cultivate inner stillness. We need to decide that we won't make a habit of using people's stories or what is said as a springboard for us to talk about something we regard as being more important, namely ourselves or what interests us. This involves our being attentive and making an effort not to be distracted. This discipline is not easy and I sometimes feel like Homer Simpson, who responded to his daughter Lisa's challenge that he wasn't listening to her with the reply: 'Just because I am not interested, doesn't mean I'm not listening!'

Sometimes we have to make a conscious effort not to feel peeved when interrupted. Early on in my Christian life, I spotted that Jesus was far less bothered than I would be when someone derailed *his* agenda. He was once on a journey to heal a centurion's daughter and I imagine him walking as fast as he could, weaving his way through the crowds when he became aware that an elderly woman had 'touched the hem of his garment' (Matthew 9:20). He could easily have walked on, regarding her as a potential diversion from his own plans. Healing a young girl was an important mission that could easily have taken priority over this woman's needs. After all, the girl was young, with life ahead of her, the woman was older; the girl was the daughter of a commander in the army, a VIP, but the woman had no social status. But Jesus is interruptible and puts his plans on hold, making space in his pressured day for this elderly woman. This story is a powerful and challenging statement about Jesus' sense of what is important. My friend Charles Whitehead, a central figure in the Catholic Charismatic Renewal, recounts a similar story about priorities and plans being changed:

> I was in India as the main speaker at a three-day conference for the local Archbishop and Mother Teresa was coming as a guest speaker on the second morning, so would arrive the previous afternoon by plane from Calcutta. She phoned to say she had so many people to take care of in Calcutta that she could not leave until the next day.
>
> The police and the Conference leaders expected thousands to come to welcome her in the afternoon and had laid on extra staff etc., accordingly so a delay was very bad news. After discussion, the airline said they would delay their last evening flight if Mother could make it much later, and so that is what happened. Mother T was adamant she could not leave those who needed her loving care under any circumstances.

She allowed the needs of people with no status to override her appointment to address the conference. Important people and prearranged plans were not her highest priority. Attending to the needs of the poor, those who really needed her, was her priority and she was not bound by her previously arranged timetable, which, as far as she was concerned, could be interrupted.

At this point, we will switch from two highly inspirational characters, Jesus and Mother Teresa, to a more mundane example of how interruptibility can apply in daily life. Imagine you are going for a walk because you want some time alone. Unfortunately, as you set off someone attempts to engage you in what might turn out to be a rather lengthy conversation. Your natural instinct might be to smile, say 'Nice day, isn't it?' and keep on walking. Yet if hospitality is a guide as to how we respond we need to ask ourselves, 'What is the most hospitable thing to do in this situation?' At this point on your walk you probably don't *feel* very hospitable, but recalling that hospitality reflects God's action towards us, you might decide, as a form of spiritual discipline, to stop and allow yourself to be interrupted. This is the sort of situation where a Rule comes into play because you have already decided to act in certain ways *before* you ever encounter that particular person. Hospitality is the deciding factor in determining your response, so you don't even need to think about whether to carry on with your walk.

It is worth noting that the main point being made here is not that other people should always determine our agenda. The issue is that we carry our pre-determined agenda lightly so that we allow others to be the centre of attention. It may not always be appropriate to allow ourselves to be interrupted, as in the case where people tried to cajole Jesus into leaving what he was doing in order to visit Lazarus.

Incorporating practices of hospitality into a Rule can help us choose the best course of action even when we may not feel like it, which is often much of the time. It helps us to exercise discipline when we might feel otherwise, and discipline is the root of the biblical concept of 'discipleship'. I actually went for a walk yesterday and several people I encountered wanted to talk, some at length. My natural impulse was to keep walking and I could easily have cut these conversations short, but I paused because the word *hospitality* was buzzing around in my mind. Many of these interactions turned out to be quite enjoyable. Of course, if I had been in a very low mood, or felt very stressed, it would have been more sensible to continue my walk without stopping; but I was feeling only moderately stressed, so I lacked a genuine excuse. A Rule can act as a guide in these seemingly small decisions, outlining for us *a way of being* that ensures we walk with God in our everyday lives, even in such mundane circumstances as going for a walk.

Making Adjustments

It is helpful to consider whether our lives are so crammed full of commitments that we have no space left to exercise hospitality. Perhaps we might have a tendency to be productive and 'to harvest right up to the very outside perimeter of any field' in our possession, not leaving anything for those who are in need. Sometimes we have very little control over our busyness, particularly if we have young children, hectic careers, or if we are caring for disabled or elderly relatives. But very often we can take more control than we might think, even if this involves our making some hard choices. Perhaps we can do less overtime than we are offered and instead visit someone who would appreciate the social contact. Or we might need, like me, to become less of a workaholic and have fewer projects on the go at any one time.

As already mentioned, we have different personalities and need to take this into account. If we easily tire in other people's company we need to ensure we have enough time alone to re-energise; only by building this recharging time into our routine will we have the capacity to practise hospitality when we do have people-contact. Only by withdrawing are we able to re-engage with people and a Rule reflects this dynamic by creating a sustainable rhythm to our lives. Some of us are more comfortable than others when it comes to taking the initiative in being hospitable. Some are great at contacting people on the telephone but I am not. The prospect of phoning someone can make me feel quite anxious. In that sense, I am not 'pastoral' and I feel stressed if I think people expect that of me - or if I expect it of myself. I feel much more comfortable when contact is spontaneous and I enjoy unplanned conversations with people in pubs or on aeroplanes. We are all different and have to work out what fits with our individual strengths and weaknesses, and what is appropriate in our own particular circumstances.

It is worth spending time to consider how we can develop hospitality practices that fit with the grain of our particular personality. Drawing an analogy from music, I sometimes think that we (our personalities) are like the instruments in a band; each instrument requires us to develop particular skills. Playing the harmonica involves our learning a very different technique from that of playing the cello (don't try blowing into a cello, it won't work). The intentional use of our personal strengths, getting the best out of ourselves, is like learning to get the best out of a musical instrument. We might, for example, come to learn how we most easily put other people at ease; it might be through our humour or it could be through creating a relaxed space in our home into which we can invite others.

The important thing is that we recognise the part hospitality plays in cultivating God's presence in our own lives and in the lives of those with whom we have contact. This gives the concept of hospitality the great dignity it deserves, as a reflection of the Gospel. Seen in this light, it is not a duty or a chore, it is not something for those of us who are good at entertaining others, as much as a spiritual practice to be embraced.

11

Proximity

The second term which characterises Celtic monasticism and its approach to people is *proximity*. Proximity indicates our closeness to, and involvement with, other people. In 1964 Marshall McLuhan introduced the now-famous phrase *'the medium is the message'*. The Gospel often needs to be seen before it is heard and we ourselves are the medium through which the message is communicated. The usual pattern in both the Gospels and in Acts is that the Good News is first demonstrated, perhaps by healing or an act of kindness, and then explained (demonstration followed by explanation).

If we are the medium through which God reveals his presence to others then our proximity is important. It is often pointed out that Christ has no hands and feet other than ours. The Bible emphasises the fact that God's presence and our presence are often synonymous. We, the Church, are described by Paul as Christ's body. Once we have cultivated his presence in our own lives we can carry his presence with us into our city streets and homes. This mirrors the action of God who, in the Incarnation, embraced proximity as a way of being (John 1:14). When we do the same it is referred to as 'the incarnational approach'.

Particularly in the West, there is a need to rethink church and mission, especially as to how we engage with our neighbours. The church can be perceived by those around us as outmoded, remote, and unrelated to everyday life. A superficial response to this challenge is to look for new programmes or techniques to engage people. I have found the Celtic emphasis on what Ian Bradley calls 'presence' - and what we are calling proximity - is of more relevance than trying the latest approach. In seeking to reframe the concept of presence for today the term 'proximity' is helpful as it refers to our distance or nearness to other people. It is a concept that helps us to consider how close we are to those around us. If there is the feeling that we are too distant then don't despair - several aspects of a Rule can help us to become more embedded in the life of our communities and embrace more of an incarnational approach to Christian living.

Finding Ways to Be Present

> Those living and working in the monasteries of the British Isles in the early medieval period expressed their Christian faith as much through being alongside people as through evangelizing them. Availability and empathy were regarded as just as valuable as missionary endeavours, if not more so.
>
> IAN BRADLEY

Members of the monastic community sought to be present in their local community in many and diverse ways, with some monasteries specialising in specific ways of engagement with the world around them. Some were primarily educational establishments, acting as major centres of scholarship and learning. Others, such as Lindisfarne and Iona, were centres of artistic creativity with monks labouring to produce wonderful illuminated manuscripts. Others acted as regional hubs establishing and maintaining satellite churches, which were nurtured under their care. Some monasteries were places where great hymns were composed and, at the other extreme, where prayers were written that could be used when milking cows. People attended monasteries at key points in their lives to seek spiritual direction. Monasteries could also be the equivalent of hospitals, places of refuge, libraries, or retreat centres. They didn't try to do it all, but each one had its own focus and occupied a particular niche. Perhaps their example can help to release contemporary churches from the burden of expectation that they should be 'all singing all dancing'.

Some monasteries were similar to the multi-purpose building favoured by many churches today, with space dedicated to worship, a cafe, a food bank, counselling rooms and a general meeting place. A friend leads a church that has an art gallery on site. The pattern of diversity in Celtic monasticism can free our imagination to envisage a variety of ways in which we too might be present in our locality, according to need. My impression is that churches as a whole generally tend to provide well for the needs of their surrounding community. The challenge is more often to do with the nature of our involvement with others as individuals, rather than as a group. This concerns our closeness, our proximity, to other people in our community.

Although some individuals were gifted evangelists, particularly those who founded monasteries, on the whole, there was more emphasis on proximity than on direct evangelism in the Celtic period. St Columba, as Ian Bradley points out, spent much of his time praying, listening, studying, and healing others. Adamnan, his biographer, presents him mainly as a prophet and healer. Donald Meeks, a sceptic of the current revival of Celtic Christianity, suggests Columba was, in fact, more of a politician than anything else. His ministry was not expressed in overt evangelism, but it did result in people coming to faith - although the suggestion that he 'converted the Picts' is likely to be an exaggeration.

Discovering how each of us might relate to others in ways that express our *unique* gifts is powerful in so many ways and we could perhaps benefit from a greater emphasis on this in our teaching. The Celtic model legitimises unity in diversity, with individuals giving expression to their particular gifts in fellowship and communion with others who have different though complementary gifts. The apostle Paul would have approved (1 Corinthians 12:21).

A Holistic Approach to Presence

For those of us in the secular West, the issue of mission has become even more challenging than it was 20 or 50 years ago. Words alone are never enough (if they ever have been). Many have recognised that what is needed is a holistic approach to the Good News of the Kingdom, where the love of God is proclaimed in both word and deed. Within evangelical circles, there can still be a false dichotomy between good works and the need to communicate the Gospel using words.

I have heard church leaders discuss with great anxiety the more recent tendency to move away from overt evangelism towards demonstrating practical care. Perhaps this drift is simply redressing an overemphasis on a particular aspect of mission within mainstream evangelicalism. Mission history suggests, that in time, practical love eventually raises questions in our neighbours and in society at large, which we will answer willingly (demonstration followed by explanation).

Alister McGrath, in *The Future of Christianity*, argues that a holistic approach was the foundation of the phenomenal growth of the church in South Korea. The involvement of Christians in political resistance to the Japanese invasion in the early twentieth century, along with the rebuilding of war-torn cities by missionaries in the second half of that century, helped people realise that God cared for their material welfare. This created an openness to the message of evangelists who followed and contributed to the remarkable growth of Christianity in South Korea. Care for the material needs of the poor was certainly a potent factor in the growth of the church in Victorian England. Those gifted in evangelism and those gifted in practical action need one another and they also need to give one another the freedom to do what each does best. It is a case of both/and not either/or.

There is good evidence that evangelism is much more effective where people are aware that those who follow Christ live sacrificially. This was one of the factors that contributed to the extraordinary growth of the Early Church; their neighbours couldn't but notice that during the plague many Christians remained in cities to look after the sick, despite the risk of infection and death (the mortality rate was 50%). Their willingness to be alongside people and care for them raised questions, providing the opportunity to explain the hope that was within them.

Sometimes Christians go to an extreme, suggesting that we don't need to share with people the Good News that God cares for them and can meet their deepest need. A quotation that is favoured is *'Preach the Gospel and use words if necessary'*. This is often attributed to St Francis but there is no evidence whatsoever that Francis ever said it. Even if he had said it, we should remember that he founded a *preaching* order. The nearest quotation from St. Francis is, 'All the Friars …should preach by their deeds', which served to remind the brothers that actions speak louder than words. By definition, we can't *proclaim* the Gospel without using words. I suspect this sentiment is promoted by people who, like me, have felt pressured into forms of evangelism that felt forced. Perhaps being more present, more alongside others, will allow us to explain our faith in the course of conversation. Proximity allows people to see our true values and to realise that we are followers of Christ, not merely religious, and curiosity can raise questions.

An emphasis on proximity/presence helps us to be alongside others in ways that are unforced, natural and authentic, in keeping with who we are as individuals. Proximity focuses on our *relationship* with those around us, rather than seeing ourselves in more functional terms - we are present as ourselves. We become available to the other, to be used in ways they might find helpful - perhaps as a listener, or a practical helper, a friend or an advisor. Even when we do have a defined role an emphasis on proximity enables us to relax, is less goal-oriented, and allows us to be more open to the reality and needs of the other person. To use Ian Bradley's words, *availability and empathy* become real possibilities when proximity is our goal.

A Theology of Friendship

Perhaps evangelism needs to be reframed, at least in Europe, where talking about religion often makes people feel awkward. It might help us to reconsider the value of genuine friendships with those who, as yet do not know the Lord. It need not be awkward when friends talk about the things they hold most dear, including our faith in God. I am certainly not a natural evangelist, but I do like it when there is an opportunity to share my faith with others, particularly when I feel God can help someone with their particular need. I have seen some remarkable things happen in the course of very simple conversations where I have implied God might be able to help that person. Friendship may be a key way to rethink proximity in today's culture, where acquaintances may be many, but friends few.

Any reflection on the nature of friendship could do worse than start with the example of Jesus. The Gospels suggest that he related to most people in a friendly, open, and compassionate way. There were some exceptions to this, particularly when he sought to confront the superior attitude of many of the Pharisees, but generally, his interactions were characterised by affection. Jesus appears to have been able to connect with a wide range of people, including some in the royal household as well as with people of disrepute. He was so blatantly hospitable and outgoing that he was criticised for being *a friend* of the wrong sort of people, tax collectors, and sinners. Jesus met people where they were, on their turf, and he joined them in their social interactions - he was labelled a glutton and drunkard by his critics because he so obviously enjoyed partaking of food and wine with others (Matthew 11:19). I don't think this means we all need to be party-lovers, as some of us are not, but the main thing to notice is that Jesus made friends with people who might not be involved in the local synagogue (read 'church' today). He most frequently related to people in everyday settings, rather than primarily in religious settings.

Spending time with 'down to earth' people and participating in their lives was not a chore for Jesus. It probably expressed a personal preference, as he, like us, was free to choose his friends. He gravitated towards the sort of people we might ourselves meet in a pub, or at a live music or sporting event and it seems that he actively enjoyed their company. Perhaps they were a friendly bunch, more welcoming than overtly religious people, such as the Pharisees, were. It has been said that Jesus was a friend of sinners for friendship's sake.

Finding Our Way Back

A year or two after becoming a Christian in my teens, I found myself involved in church activities five nights each week, which left little space for my old friendship network. I would have had to abandon lots of my church activities, including cleaning the church and helping with children's work, to have reconnected with my old friends. In retrospect, my over-involvement removed me from a context where I could naturally share my faith. No longer being part of my former social networks meant that evangelism became a duty and it required the confidence and bravado of a salesman, which I have never possessed.

When this sort of abstraction process happens Christians feel that they *ought* to evangelise, so they venture out on 'raiding parties', leaving the safety of 'the fort' for evangelistic forays into the local community, before beating a hasty retreat back to the safety of the palisade. Some churches train believers to go into the streets and have a word of knowledge about a stranger's needs. I am fully supportive of using spiritual gifts outside church settings but the main issue here is that if we had closer relationships with unchurched people in the first place, we would not need a spiritual gift to know their needs - they would have told us and they might have actually asked us to pray for them.

Whilst speaking at a conference for church leaders I was recently asked how to mobilise people to 'take up their responsibility for evangelism'. My response was that we should help people take up their responsibility to love those around and encourage them to do this in their own way. If we focus too much on evangelism it makes many Christians feel guilty. I talked about the extraction process outlined above, how churches remove people from their existing networks and channel their enthusiasm into church-based projects. I am not sure whether my answer was good or not, but I do think church leaders need to rethink this process.

Would we be happy to say to most people, as did Jesus, '**Go home to your friends** and tell them how much the Lord has done for you...' (Mark 5:19)? I imagine this formerly demonised man returned to his old friends, who had most likely given up all hope of ever seeing him again. I also imagine that they asked him what had happened. He didn't have to find a way to turn the conversation to the things of God, because he was the talk of the town. All he needed to do was to reconnect with his community and respond to people's questioning, which is what is meant by being 'a witness'.

Churches do need to become strong communities because they are places where we are formed and supported as disciples, but when churches extract us from most other relationships, it removes us from the very context in which God wants us to outwork our discipleship. We can easily end up living in a ghetto with church involvement becoming all-consuming. A gated existence then replaces our ability to be a Christian presence in our neighbourhood. When we lose proximity we may be quite unaware that we now inhabit a Christian ghetto, because it seems so normal and might even be promoted as being a good thing, a sign of commitment, or as indicating that we are 'not of the world'.

In 1986 we planted a church in a village in Somerset, in the Southwest of England. We were a relatively small church but ended up running two youth clubs, a children's ministry, a nutritional programme for deprived young people, home groups, a parent and toddler group, occasional Alpha courses and more. It was an active church, but in retrospect, I suspect that we were too active. We were doing a lot for our community, but people from our locality rarely ever started conversations about God.

When we moved location and started another church we were determined to have a different approach. Rather than run projects, we joined in more with activities already going on in our local community. It came as quite a surprise just how many of our unchurched friends and acquaintances have started God-conversations, quite unprompted. This approach is more a case of 'participating in' what already exists in our locality - being *in* the world - than 'providing for'. I am not suggesting that running church-based projects or ministries is, in any way, a bad thing - it is a fantastic way of serving our community and increasingly church-based projects are vital for people's welfare - but we can easily overlook other, more natural ways to engage with people. Friendship provides the context in which today we will most often be asked to explain the hope that is within us (1 Peter 3:15-16).

Please note what is *not being* advocated here: the idea is not to develop friendships where the real motive for getting to know someone is evangelism. If we adopt this approach we can end up forming relationships with others - which is good - but we have an ulterior motive - which is sneaky. Friendship is great and it seems to me that if we love our friends we will want them to have the same security in God that we have but it seems odd to form friendships as a strategy, rather than because we want someone's friendship for its own sake. This is an example of what has been called 'bait and switch', where we promise one thing, friendship, but our real motivation is not friendship per se; it is evangelism. Bait and switch is not the best way to address our failure to be rooted in a place, in a community and everyday relationships.

Resisting Objectifying Others

Sometimes we are encouraged in sermons, talks and books to develop relationships with specific *groups* of people. If we are white and middle class we might be exhorted to relate more to working-class people or perhaps to members of other racial groups. There is some merit in this and some of us do experience a specific call to bring the love of God, in word and action, to specific ethnic groups or particular cultural tribes. At times we do need encouragement to look beyond stereotypes and begin genuinely to value other people for who they are. But berating the church for its lack of outreach to those who are culturally distant objectifies other people. We see an individual as a target for our actions and relate to them simply because they belong to a specific group (the poor or a particular ethnic group etc.) It is better to relate to other people because we genuinely like them, enjoy their company, or respect them as individuals. They might have obvious needs that we care about or they might seem fairly sorted, but we have a desire to know them better.

Friendship does not mean that we simply choose to relate to people like us and we need to be open to being drawn to those who are different. Exploring diversity can be fascinating, an opportunity to learn from others and be changed for the better as a result of our interaction with them. God often draws us to certain people and when that happens we expect that there will be mutual benefit.

Sometimes Christians withdraw from contact with neighbours or work colleagues because they disagree over politics, gender issues, or issues of morality. It is, of course, good to avoid the company of those who might draw us away from God or lead us back into a previously harmful lifestyle, but sometimes our withdrawal is simply motivated by the desire to surround ourselves with like-minded people who present no challenge whatsoever to our worldview. I have noticed this tendency on both sides of the Atlantic.

The Apostle Paul advocated withdrawal in certain circumstances, but he has been seriously misunderstood on this matter: 'I wrote you in my letter not to associate with sexually immoral persons - **not at all meaning** the immoral of this world, or the greedy and robbers, or idolaters...' (1 Corinthians 5:9-10). He advised the Corinthian Church to distance themselves from people who advocated free love under the name of Christianity but not to withdraw from contact with non-believers. He goes on to tell the Corinthians not to judge people outside the Faith, presumably because their lifestyle was the result of their being unenlightened - on top of which they are subject to strong pressures and temptations without the power of the Holy Spirit within to resist. There is a difference between our being set apart for God (holy) and becoming a holy huddle.

Giving & Receiving

We have seen that Celtic monasteries were centres for what we might now describe as social care ministry. Since its inception, the church has always sought to meet people's material and physical needs. Even the earliest missionary ventures of the disciples included the commandment to 'heal the sick' - forerunners of those who through the ages have had a healing ministry, as well as more recent medical missionaries (Luke 10:9). As churches and organisations, we want to do all we can to alleviate suffering and indeed we do.

The Covid crisis has left many people reliant on food banks and BBC news, regional and national, has frequently featured churches involved in this ministry - in the UK the Church is the major provider of food banks. But alongside our giving to others, we also need to be able to receive. This was something very much recognised by Mother Teresa, who in an interview in 1977, said,

> The poor give us much more than we give them. They're such strong people, living day to day with no food. And they never curse, never complain. We don't have to give them pity or sympathy. We have so much to learn from them.

If the traffic is all one-way people end up feeling that they don't themselves have anything to give, or worse, they may feel patronised. The range of ways in which we serve others is truly wonderful so please don't take this as a criticism of our efforts, but it can be off-putting when the Church is seen as being self-sufficient, not needing what others have to offer. This might seem to be an odd point to make in a chapter describing what we, the Church, have to give to other people, but it is often overlooked. Jesus received people's friendship and enjoyed their hospitality. The home of Lazarus, Martha and Mary was somewhere he seemed able to relax and talk. Being the recipient of hospitality is a way of giving dignity to those offering it, acknowledging implicitly that we welcome or need what they have to offer us. Receiving from others suggests that we are dependent on *their* generosity, which can be quite a challenge for those of us who need constantly to adopt a giving stance.

We might even consider that receiving from others is a form of spiritual discipline, an expression of our dependency on God. It is interesting that, as Jesus pointed out, Elijah was sent to receive help from a widow living in the land where Baal was worshipped (Luke 4:26). She was someone we might disqualify on three counts: she had few resources, she was of low status and she was not one of God's people. But Elijah needed her, and once God's provision at the Brook Cherith had dried up he became reliant on her generosity (1 Kings 17:10-11).

John 4, the story of the woman at the well, illustrates the mutuality of giving and receiving. Here we see Jesus interacting with an outsider, someone from a group despised by his own religious group. The conversation was motivated by the fact that he needed *her* help - he was thirsty but had no bucket to access the water. Contact was initiated on the basis of *his* need. This led to an interaction where there was mutual benefit, giving and receiving. A certain degree of banter developed, suggesting Jesus was enjoying the conversation, perhaps he was even having fun. This interaction, I suggest, must have been affectionate rather than judgmental, otherwise she would have felt condemned when he told her the details of her murky past and would have returned to her village shamed. Clearly, this was not the case. What was initially an open and possibly playful conversation created an interesting opportunity to talk about faith. But the basis of this interaction was their mutual need of each other. Jesus needed the woman at the well to help him and we may find ourselves in need of help from others.

Our Presence & God's Presence

In a similar vein, in sending out his disciples in the mission given to them, Jesus instructed them to *receive* hospitality from those to whom they were sent (Luke 10:5-8). As they travelled around these early disciples embraced a form of voluntary poverty. They became dependent on the generosity of others, similar to the mendicant - begging - friars of the middle ages who were dependent on the charity of others. In one passage Jesus suggests that when a person welcomes a disciple they are, in fact, welcoming him (Matthew 10:40). This is further reinforced by the way Jesus equated a negative reaction to the disciples with a negative response to himself (John 15:18-20). It has always struck me that Paul was told that he was persecuting Jesus, when in fact he was persecuting his followers (Acts 9:4). People are not just reacting to us personally - their attitude towards us mirrors their attitude to God, whose presence we carry and whose likeness we bear.

In 2 Corinthians 3:18, the Apostle Paul makes an extraordinary claim. He attributes great power to the time we spend contemplating God's glory. He tells us that our experience of God's presence, through the Spirit, has the power to transform us so that we carry with us that same glory, the same presence, in our own lives: 'And we all, with unveiled faces, beholding the glory of the Lord, are being transformed into the same image (eikon) from one degree of glory to another'. The word he uses, eikon, is the term from which we get 'icon'.

Paul doesn't explain the dynamic of this transformation, but it is clearly a continual process of change - the result is that you and I become an image of the holy. We come to reflect God's glory in the same way that the moon reflects the light of the sun. Paul is referring to Moses, who spent time in God's presence on the mountain and whose face continued to glow with God's glory as he descended into the valley. Cultivating God's presence in our own lives results in a visible change, which can be seen by the people around us. We carry God's glory with us into new situations.

A friend recently took a taxi from a train station. The driver, to her great surprise, asked her if she was a Christian. The reason was that a church had started providing free hot drinks for taxi drivers and others working at night in very cold weather. The driver said she was just like those people.

I find the fact that we are being transformed is reassuring, particularly at those times when I feel that my influence for good is minimal. Although we are often unaware that we have been changed through our contact with God, it is, according to Paul, a given; if we spend time in God's presence we will inevitably carry something of that presence with us. The presence of the indwelling Holy Spirit is the basis of Paul's teaching that we are Christ's body, his visible presence on earth (1 Corinthians 12). In my early days, I picked up the feeling that we need to represent God to those around us by being very careful, deliberate and on our guard. I recall singing a song which made me feel vaguely paranoid: 'They are watching you and the things you do, hearing the things that you say. Let them see the Saviour as he shines in you...' The thought that my unchurched friends were watching me was not at all comforting! This was reminiscent of the song 'I'll be watching you' by The Police - a song popular at weddings even though the real topic of the song is stalking and the desire to induce anxiety in the person being watched! The idea of our being transformed into God's presence is much less fraught.

Carrying God's glory can be unself-conscious, a natural process rather than something we strain to do. When we take proximity seriously we become those who carry God's presence to our friends and neighbours, expressed in the words of Godfrey Birtill's song *Looking for Your Presence*:

Carrying You ... Carrying You
Into the city streets and homes.
Carrying You ... Carrying You
We hear the footsteps of the Lord.

12

Places

Cultivating the presence of God can have a profound impact on us as individuals, as well as on those around us. In addition to its effect on people, this cultivation process can result in a tangible sense of God's presence in the *places* where we live, worship, work or study. I first experienced this for myself at Ffald y Brenin.

Many people have reported remarkable experiences of God whilst on retreat at Ffald y Brenin. This has been the case since its inception, but in the mid-2000s there was an increased sense of God's presence, particularly in the chapel, some of which is carved out of the bare rock of the Welsh hills. In 2006 when leading a retreat at the centre for a group of church leaders, I went into the chapel to sit quietly. The presence of God was so intense that I found it difficult to stay there for more than 15 minutes. It is difficult to describe this experience, but it was similar to the experience I had had at my conversion; wonderful but quite overwhelming. If I had stayed in that atmosphere any longer it would have been very difficult for me to re-engage with leading a retreat.

Ffald y Brenin retreat centre is a place where people often come to find God's presence. God is regularly invited to be present during times of prayer, along with intercession and speaking blessing over the community - all under the guidance of the Holy Spirit. The desire for this experience to be replicated more widely has given rise to the *Local Houses of Prayer* movement (LHOPs). Ffald y Brenin's LHOPs are now an active presence in many nations as an outflow of the river of the vision, life and practices of the centre.

This heightened sense of God's presence can similarly be cultivated in our homes through regular and ongoing prayer and this sometimes spills over into our communities, mirroring the experience at the retreat centre. Recently a friend told me that an unchurched neighbour had heard that she was praying for their neighbourhood and had asked her how long that had been happening, as she felt that there had been a marked change in the atmosphere in their street.

Thin Places

> How awesome is this place! This is none other than the house of God, and this is the gate of heaven.
> GENESIS 28:17

The thought that there are certain *places* where God is more easily experienced has not always found universal favour. For those of us in the evangelical tradition the thought that God's presence might be made more tangible in particular places doesn't quite fit our theology. We emphasise that church is a community, not a building and that God dwells in people, rather than in bricks and mortar - but nevertheless, we have to admit that some church buildings which have been soaked in prayer, *do feel* different. Many of us have had the experience of visiting homes, churches or retreat centres where God seems to infuse the atmosphere. There is an openness to the idea that God's presence is more evident in particular places at particular times, as in the case of revival. In addition, Christians from Pentecostal and Charismatic traditions especially will often travel to churches (such as the Toronto Airport Church in the mid-1990s), as well as to retreat centres such as Ffald y Brenin, where they believe God is more easily encountered. Of course, Catholic and Orthodox believers have always had their special 'holy' sites of pilgrimage, so perhaps the rest of us are simply catching up with what has been obvious to them all along.

Just to reassure those who may be unfamiliar with this concept; it is the *spiritual atmosphere,* rather than the bricks and mortar, which changes through ongoing prayer and faithful Christian living. It is this sort of change in the atmosphere which is linked to the concept of a 'thin place'. No one can be certain who first used this term but it seems to have originated in Celtic regions and it has been taken up with some enthusiasm by those exploring Celtic Christianity. A thin place is somewhere where there has been a history of believers having consistently engaged in spiritual practices, with the result that the divide between earthly reality and heaven seems to be almost negligible. How this works defies rational analysis, but it is nonetheless real.

As mentioned, the concept of a thin place emerged from the worldview of the ancient Celts. They did not view the world as existing in three layers, with heaven above, the place of the dead (hades) below and earth in the middle. For them, heaven, God's dwelling place, was not somewhere 'up there'. They believed that heaven and earth, the physical and spiritual, coexist, occupying the same space, rather than being separate and distant realms. They realised that everything physical has a spiritual component and that everything spiritual has a physical counterpart.

The physical reality around us usually fills our senses, occupying the foreground of our awareness, so that the coexistent spiritual reality remains hidden in the background. When the surrounding spiritual reality comes into sharper focus, we are in a thin place. We see through the barrier between the physical and spiritual realms. God becomes more real to us, an experience usually accompanied by a sense of awe, or sometimes profound drowsiness. A thick veil often hides the spiritual realm from our eyes, but now there is only a thin transparent veil. This describes Jacob's experience at Bethel, where he became intensely aware of God's presence. Eventually, Bethel became a shrine, a permanent site, where people would go to meet with God. Jacob is not the only biblical example where the veil between heaven and earth becomes 'thin'. Elisha's servant had a similar experience when he and his master were surrounded by a hostile enemy. He became aware of the spiritual reality surrounding them and could clearly see the vast angelic army on the hills around them, easily outnumbering their foes (2 Kings 6:17).

Architecture

Once we become aware of the existence of thin places we find that they are not at all uncommon. We had a garden room built three years ago. It was intended to be an art room but has been used more often as a place to pray. Sometimes we pray there alone, sometimes with others. We often have a sense of God's presence on entering the garden room. There is a depth of peace, tranquillity, which goes beyond the fact that it is a pleasant space. Others have reported similar experiences where they regularly pray in a particular part of their home. Our garden room is for us the equivalent of a monastic cell.

There are two primary types of monastic architecture, the cell and the monastery and it is worth considering both. Celtic monasteries, the first type, were regarded as being 'God's turf'. Ian Bradley, in *Colonies of Heaven*, describes how it was believed that upon entering the monastery grounds, a person actually became physically present in the kingdom of God. In this view, the monastery was effectively an outpost of heaven, a place where God was honoured and obeyed. Paul writes to the church in Philippi, which was itself a Roman colony, in similar terms (Philippians 3:20).

A colony consisted of settlers who fully intended to live out their lives in that place. Roman colonists, such as those at Philippi, were permanent residents, never intending to go home to Rome. In this case, they were soldiers who, as a reward for their service, had been settled in Philippi but their allegiance remained primarily to Rome. They were colonists because they lived under the rule of Rome and submitted to its laws and authority, even though they lived at a distance from Rome. Celtic monks similarly regarded a monastery as a place wholly under the rule of another king. In similar vein Christian homes and communities, infused with prayer and practical discipleship, form an outpost, a colony, of heaven - they become specific locations where God rules.

A cell is the second type of monastic architecture. It can be part of a monastic enclosure, but it can also be an individual self-contained living space. Alternatively, separate cells could be built to form small clusters with monks and/or nuns living in close proximity, as a forerunner to the monastery. The cell remains of utmost importance to monastic life, as it embodies the paradoxical combination of restriction (it is small) with the endless possibility for learning more about oneself and God. The Russian Orthodox Church introduced the term *Poustinia*, which means desert, to describe a cabin or a room where one goes to pray. This has inspired many people to set aside a particular room, or a corner of a room, as the place where they engage with prayer and Bible reading, repurposing the idea of a monastic cell for ordinary people.

Homes as Monastic Cells

'Zacchaeus, hurry and come down, for I must stay at your house today.' So he hurried and came down and received him joyfully.
LUKE 19: 5-6.

Zacchaeus was an outsider whom we encounter perched halfway up a tree, trying to get a view of Jesus as he passed by. In these rather unusual circumstances, Jesus singled him out and initiated a relationship with him. It is important to notice that in the subsequent interaction Jesus related to Zacchaeus as a person *who is located in a particular place*; he asked to come to that place, his home. People are important to God, but so are the places we inhabit. Jesus wept over Jerusalem - a place with a history, an ancient site which was the location of a specific community.

Anne de Leyser is the director of the Local Houses of Prayer network. She went on a retreat to Ffald y Brenin retreat centre because she had read about the encounters with God which people had experienced there. Her first visit to the centre did not result in a dramatic encounter (and this has also been her experience on subsequent visits). In her own words: 'I did not experience a weightiness of the presence of God at that time. To be honest I was quite struck by the ordinariness'. On returning home she noticed a stronger sense of God's presence there, experiencing more of the weight of God's glory. Some more spectacular events followed and on one occasion large flakes of silver and gold appeared on the carpet as her husband was praying. Anne is unable to explain the dynamics behind this experience, but she believes that even though her time at the centre was outwardly quite unspectacular, something actually happened when she was on retreat there.

Anne's story illustrates two things: the first is that there are ancient places where prayer has changed the spiritual climate. These are places where we can imbibe God's presence, even when there are no outward signs at the time. The second thing her story illustrates is how our homes can be transformed as we pray and become a form of monastic cell.

Imagine the potential if people with little personal experience of Church were to experience God's presence for themselves as they enter our homes, even if they may not be able to articulate what they feel. Our Christian friends could also be drawn deeper into God presence when they enter houses which have become a place of prayer. Imagine if through prayer and ongoing involvement a similar, gradual, transformation occurred in our street or at our place of work.

Geography is Important

The idea that God might tangibly be present in a particular place can seem novel to us in the West because often we regard ourselves primarily as individuals, whose greatest purpose in life is to realise our full potential. Yet we only have to read the repeated references to specific locations in the Old Testament to realise that we have lost the sense that God is concerned with places as well as people. He is interested in our geography, not just our in our psychology and personal well-being.

An emphasis on the importance of place has in fact been revived in theological circles in recent years, with several books having been written on the topic. A course I once tutored included studying both the 'theology of place' and the importance of hospitality. One student was living in a block of flats (a condominium) surrounded by unchurched neighbours, most of whom were strangers to one another. The usual trajectory for the residents was that they would stay there for as short a time as possible before moving on to somewhere better. The student decided to focus on the place where he lived and to practise hospitality. In time one neighbour said to him that in the natural course of events he would at that point be moving on, but had decided to stay because of the depth of community he had experienced there. This story alerts us to the possibility of communities being transformed so that the place where we live or work might become a thin place.

We need to consider certain cultural shifts which work against our cultivating God's presence in a particular place. A significant number of us fail to realise the importance given in Scripture to being embedded in our community (town, village or a city neighbourhood). Communities are the places where we recognise others and our name is known. It is,

135

however, an emphasis that can be at odds with the way a modern industrial society works, particularly among the well-educated, more wealthy, mobile population who value career progression. David Goodhart makes a distinction between 'Anywheres' and 'Somewheres' in a recent book on the nature of society (*The Road to Somewhere*). 'Anywheres' are often highly educated people with many opportunities to live and work in various locations; they rarely put down deep roots in one place. 'Somewheres' often live and work within a short distance of where they were born and they have a strong sense that they belong to that particular place and that the place belongs to them. Of course, this is a generalisation, as Anywheres often decide to put down roots towards middle age or retirement, but it does help us to become aware of our own approach to the place where we live. Is our home, and our neighbourhood, a dormitory where we just sleep and eat, or is it the base for us to be an integral part of our local community? A further factor to consider is the shift that has occurred in the West where we seek for that elusive commodity 'space', rather than place.

Place vs Space

The importance of actual places is emphasised much less today than it was in the past and instead, we hear more about our need for 'space'. The sociologist Zygmunt Bauman highlighted this in his book *Community: Seeking Safety in an Insecure World*. He suggests that we have replaced what he considers to be a more healthy focus on place with a need for 'space'. Space is shorthand for our longing for independence; it is finding release from the sorts of commitments which arise when we are deeply rooted in the particular places where we live, socialise and work. Bauman's views resonate with those of St Benedict, who held a disdain for the previously mentioned wandering monks who fail to commit to a particular place. These monks visit, rather than join, communities and have no common Rule - instead, they make up a Rule for themselves, to ensure a lifestyle of freedom from restraint.

Community brings a degree of security, but the trade-off we make, in being part of a community, is that we inevitably develop attachments and commitments to other people. This creates a sense of responsibility and we lose some of our independence. Those who are successful in finding 'space' often do so by living in gated pseudo-communities. This maintains a fragile sense of security by shutting out those parts of their world which, although close by, they wish to ignore. We see this in both cities and villages where the wealthy and the poor inhabit different communal areas. Often these areas abut one another, but the inhabitants of each rarely interact at any depth.

This pursuit of space can also involve owning a second home to escape from everyday demands. This is not always a bad thing, but it can represent a transient and detached existence, especially when second homeowners fail to integrate with the local community. Bauman highlights how our quest for space does deliver a sense of independence, but the cost is often loneliness, isolation and a feeling of insecurity.

Place is necessary to form a fully orbed community, in which people are known in depth. Today we refer to people with common traits or interests as a community, so that we might, for example, refer to the 'Artistic community'. But most of those who are considered part of such 'communities' never actually meet one another so this seems rather dubious. Of course, we can form virtual online communities which are meaningful and this is a good alternative to being wholly isolated. But our ability to truly encounter others online is limited unless we know them in other settings; we get to know people by experiencing them in everyday situations. I am not convinced that we can say we belong to *the* Church, without belonging to *a* church in a locality - and note that mutuality is implied by the word 'belong'. Similarly, we can imagine ourselves to be part of the global village but play no part in the life of a small village. These are alternatives to genuine community, what Bauman calls communities 'of non-belonging, a togetherness of loners'. We have the illusion of belonging but without the discomfort of being bound by the obligations and commitments which genuine community brings.

The Challenge

God settles the solitary in a home...
PSALM 68:6

Locatedness, being deeply embedded in a locality, is an essential ingredient to what it means to be fully human. A realisation of the importance of place - and our being rooted - brings us back to the often-messy reality of our own lives and our communities. We are faced with the need to learn how best to live alongside an unpleasant neighbour, an opinionated church member or an overly demanding friend. Once we learn to prioritise place over 'space' we gain a fresh sense of calling to this particular town, this particular church and this set of friends, even when none of these seems ideal. We realise, in the words of Psalm 68, that God has settled us in a home so we determine to stick at it. This realisation creates wonderful possibilities.

The dream of our home becoming a thin place becomes a genuine possibility once we grasp the fact that this place is *my* place, and it is a location that is genuinely important to God. Our homes become the plot of land where we begin to slowly cultivate God's presence, applying the insights we have gleaned from monastic spirituality. We come to realise that the presence of God is cultivated by our rather simple times of prayer, alone and together with others.

Our persistent prayer for, and ongoing interaction with, our neighbours can begin to change the atmosphere. We become more practised at performing acts of hospitality, at remaining humble, being vulnerable and so on. Seemingly unspectacular practices such as these bear fruit. What is more, this is within reach of ordinary people, not something for especially enlightened Christians - a far cry from a quick-fix approach which promises 'the secret of spiritual success'. God's preference is that we remain weak and unsophisticated as we outwork these things (he tends to confound the strong and outwit the wise).

So the challenge is this: are we committed to a particular place? Have we let ourselves become deeply embedded in the community where we live? Are our homes a 'thin place', or at least on the way to becoming one? Is there a sense that our Christian communities (churches) are colonies of heaven, rooted in our city but representing the rule of another place? Do we believe that through hospitality, prayerful attentiveness and so on we will see God's reign more evidently present in our towns, villages and cities?

Yet this emphasis on the importance of place is not always an easy path. It brings us to the importance of what The Rule of Benedict refers to as *stability* - sticking with challenging situations and navigating relationships with people whom we find difficult rather than deciding to 'cut and run'.

Persistence in One Place

> The Rule of Benedict is... all about staying in the same place with the same people. The height of self-denial is not hair shirts and all-night vigils: it's standing next to the same person quietly for years on end.
> ROWAN WILLIAMS (THE WAY OF ST BENEDICT)

Benedictine vows affirm a commitment to a particular place (monastery) with its particular community of monks or nuns, warts and all. The vow to remain in one monastery for life means that monks and nuns have to learn how to persevere with the challenges of living in community when, inevitably, difficulties arise between people. When we flee from community we are often running away from ourselves and stability becomes a strategy for personal growth. If we stick at things the only viable option is to learn how to be open and honest, working through differences and seeking healthy compromises.

Many of us embark on commitments to people and places but have a get-out clause just in case the going gets tough, as it inevitably does - we ensure that the backdoor is kept open. But changing location avoids the opportunity for us to become more authentic. Deep down we know that moving on won't work forever - we either have to engage with what is around us or live the life of a wanderer, as in the case of Cain (Genesis 4:12).

Most of us will never make a vow of stability in quite the same way that a Benedictine monk would, but we can consider making *lifelong* commitments, to friends, people, ministries and places. Although this puts constraints on us, it puts us in good company as Jesus similarly limited himself. He never travelled outside a small Middle Eastern country and he mostly confined his ministry to just one ethnic group - these constraints, these commitments, resulted in great effectiveness.

Jesus chose to embrace limitations rather than seek to escape them. He resisted the temptation to spread himself thinly, even when he realised just how intensely frustrating his actual friends could be.

Instead, he committed himself to their development, focusing on twelve, three of whom became his closest friends. It is sobering to realise that when he died there were only 120 in his 'church' (Acts 1:15). His disciples had more freedom to travel and they ended up travelling much further than he ever did. He engaged with what was in front of him, fully embracing the present and ignored the greener grass which was further afield. He could hardly be said to have pursued the extensive, more exciting ministry that many hanker after today.

Idealism vs Realism

Dietrich Bonhoeffer, master of the provocative phrase, wrote that 'God hates visionary dreamers'! He was referring to people who embrace the concept of community, but who cut and run when faced with the reality of an actual community. No community is likely to ever correspond to our ideal notion of what a community 'should' look like. Bonhoeffer suggested that we can fall in love with a concept and then demand that God and others make our dream come true. The reality is that the people who form a community never quite measure up to the vision of those of us who know how a community 'should' operate (which is where the term 'dreamers' comes in).

Visionary dreamers tend to be enthusiastic early on, but they inevitably move on, often leaving a trail of criticism behind them. It is also unlikely that visionary dreamers will settle with a particular Rule (it won't be good enough). Their process of engagement is likely to follow a pattern described in psychological terms as *idealisation* in the early stages - 'this is just what I have been looking for' - followed by *denigration* - 'I now realise that you don't practise what you preach'. Anyone who has been in a church long enough will recognise this pattern - in themselves or in others. But once we see the value of stability our approach can change as we come to recognise that we need first and foremost to work on ourselves, not on the community.

The enemy of stability is the idea that the grass is greener on the other side. Sometimes it is greener, but more often it simply looks better from a distance - up close it is just the same old grass. I am not thinking here of situations of abuse, where we need to leave to avoid further damage.

In that instance, we should flee, but otherwise, we can at least consider staying put and giving things a second chance. Stability forces us to tend to the grass around us in an attempt to make it greener. If we develop the habit of having an escape plan, 'just in case...', we will keep a part of ourselves in reserve and never fully engage with others or with our locality in a wholehearted manner.

Place & Growth

We have an impact on a place or a community but, in turn, that place also has an impact on us. This is not always easy since engagement often makes us feel vulnerable - what if they don't like me? what if I prove to be ineffective? - but engagement *can* lead to personal growth and change. Furthermore, strained relationships with those in our church, family or social group make community life difficult. We can end up trying to avoid particular people because they are a challenge but the underlying issue is sometimes that those particular people don't respond to the ways we have developed to manage interactions.

We all develop certain strategies to get others to do what we want but to succeed we require others to conform and play ball. When they don't conform, it is as if the music has started but they refuse to dance. For instance, if someone is dominant, talkative and opinionated, our usual ploy might be to smile, nod agreeably and hope that our kindness will change them for the better - but when this avoidant strategy doesn't work we have to dig deeper into what is behind our own particular behaviour. Is it that I avoid honest interactions with others, frightened that openness will cause conflict? Perhaps we need to learn to be more upfront and realise that we can be more robust without being rude or offensive. Stability helps us grow, although it is not an easy option.

If we are constantly on the move we simply transplant any problems we are facing. As Amma Matrona, one of the Desert Mothers, said, 'We carry ourselves wherever we go'. Rather than address any root issues we hope a move will sort things out. We 'do a geographical', as it is known in Alcoholics Anonymous. Actual places and particular communities can help us grow and change for the better.

Place & Pilgrimage

In this chapter, we have looked at the importance of physical places and the communities which inhabit them. The Celtic idea of a 'thin place' is an encouragement to pray and to pursue other spiritual practices which cultivate God's presence in our homes and communities. Benedict's concept of stability has also been explored. Of course, stability might seem to be at odds with the Celtic approach of pilgrimage. Celtic Christians put weight on an adventurous form of discipleship, which meant that some would leave their monasteries and venture forth - but for many, their pilgrimage took the form of journeying with Jesus in their ongoing discipleship in one particular place.

To reconcile the concepts of stability and pilgrimage it is necessary to attempt to discern what is at the heart of both of these ideas. Stability is above all a way of ensuring that we don't easily give up when difficulties arise. Stability flags up the need for persistence, highlighting the folly of always pursuing the illusion of something better. There is a story of a monk going to Abbot Moses, one of the Desert Fathers, for advice. The abbot told him: 'Go to your cell, and your cell will teach you everything'. The limitation of the monastic cell - or whatever equivalent limitations we face - forces us to confront the person who occupies the cell, me. Today we value gaining experience in different settings and travel can indeed broaden the mind, but we ignore Abbot Moses' wisdom at our peril.

Stability underlines the value of perseverance in a culture that wants it all and wants it now. To re-contextualise this today we need to ensure that we are stable people, not easily knocked off course and not prone to seeking the latest teaching or the most exciting church. We can be butterfly hunters, chasing after the latest ephemeral Christian novelty, in the hope that it will instantly transform our lives. I would suggest that it is legitimate for us to consider moving location unless we feel a clear call to remain in a particular area - but it helps if we can carefully evaluate our motives for such a move. We are likely to achieve more through long-term relationships with particular people and particular places than we are through constantly moving.

Pilgrimage can be the symptom of a restless personality and stability brings a helpful balance in that regard. On the other hand, pilgrimage can result from a deeply felt desire to respond to the will of God and a call to live with uncertainty - it can be the outworking of love and trust. Pilgrimage can result in our finding a new location where, like St Columba, we will put down deep roots. Having deep roots allows us to cultivate God's presence in that place so that in time our place will become a thin place.

Part Four

Renewing Ancient Practices

'COULD IT BE THAT IN THE POST-MODERN, PICK-AND-MIX SPIRITUAL SUPERMARKET WE NOW INHABIT, PEOPLE ARE ACTUALLY CRAVING COMMITMENT, DISCIPLINE AND OBEDIENCE? WHAT AT FIRST SIGHT MIGHT SEEM TO BE ONE OF THE LEAST APPEALING ASPECTS OF THE MONASTERIUM MODEL TO MODERN CHRISTIANS IS PERHAPS AN INCREASINGLY POSITIVE ATTRACTION.'

IAN BRADLEY
COLONIES OF HEAVEN

'A RULE OF LIFE SHOULD BE FLEXIBLE ENOUGH TO ADJUST TO THE REALITIES OF A PERSON'S LIFE BUT FIRM ENOUGH TO REQUIRE OBEDIENCE.'

GREG PETERS
THE STORY OF MONASTICISM

13

Patterns of Prayer

To briefly recap what has been covered so far: initially, we looked at how we become more aware of God's presence at particular times, with certain people and in certain places. This is described by the theological term 'immanence', an awareness that God is near at hand. Awareness of God is heightened in times of revival, but here our focus has been how to cultivate a more sustained experience of his presence.

We have looked at how particular attitudes, practices, and patterns of behaviour play a part in paving the way for us to experience God. Passages in Scripture such as 'The friendship of the Lord is for those who fear him' (Psalm 25:14) support this idea and Celtic and other forms of monasticism have provided us with clues as to how we might approach this today.

This fourth section examines some of the ingredients considered essential in developing a Rule for today. A Rule integrates individual spiritual disciplines into a more complete way of life by creating a rhythm of work, worship, rest and recreation. The balance of these elements is considered subsequently but here we start with a closer look at prayer since it forms the foundation for a monastic rhythm.

Establishing a Rhythm of Prayer

This chapter builds upon what has already been described as 'prayerful attentiveness' whilst recognising that prayer is a broader topic than the still-small-voice, contemplative, type of prayer that we considered earlier. Praying several times each day reorientates us by repeatedly making space for us to experience God's presence. Prayer creates the opportunity to hear his still small voice. In addition, when we regularly use words of Scripture in our prayers, it grounds us in the truth of, for example, God's steadfast love and faithfulness. When we pray verses such as Lamentations 3:24 we remind ourselves that God is indeed trustworthy: 'The Lord is my portion, says my soul. Therefore, I will hope in Him'. Repeating such a prayer reinforces the fact that life is never completely hopeless. A verse I have prayed many times is: 'May the beauty of the Lord be upon us, establish thou the work of our hands', part of a psalm used in *Celtic Daily Prayer* at Midday Prayer. I believe that God hears us and that our efforts will bear more fruit as we pray this verse from Psalm 90. Try it - it really does seem that God blesses our work in new ways when we ask him repeatedly to 'establish' it.

Having a rhythm of prayer changes us, the *'pray-ers'*, as well as affecting the situations we pray for. In addition, the *place* where we pray can become a 'thin place' as God's presence becomes more tangible in our homes or church buildings - the spiritual atmosphere changes when a place is soaked in prayer. If we prayer-walk our streets that can also affect the spiritual climate of our neighbourhood.

The key to this is persistence, more like engaging in a long steady walk than sprinting. If we pray, day after day, that God will bless our neighbours' work, their families and their homes, we might be surprised at the result. Jesus advocated this form of persistent prayer, citing the example of a widow who continually petitioned a judge to act on her behalf - he acts purely because she keeps pestering him (Luke 18:1-8)! The message is clear: keep on asking, never give up. It is perhaps a mystery why regular intercession is often required, as God hears our initial prayer, but experience shows this to be the case.

Beyond the Traditional QT

I have never found prayer easy. My mind tends to wander, especially when I see a new email arriving or when there is a guitar nearby, begging to be played. There are many books on my desk, all waiting to be read.

In short, distractions are everywhere, so I need a structure to help me to persist in prayer.

For much of my life prayer has taken the shape of a traditional QT, the 'quiet time' advocated in evangelical circles. This combines Bible reading with prayers of adoration, confession, thanksgiving and supplication (which can be remembered by the acronym ACTS). The QT was often hard work and quite demanding in terms of the mental effort as, without any set prayers, I had to keep thinking about what to pray. Despite this, I found it helpful so I persisted with this approach for many years until I discovered the existence of other approaches to devotional life.

The monastic practice of praying by using the Psalms was one such important discovery and represents a powerful way to engage with God. The Psalms, the hymnbook of ancient Israel, contain songs and prayers which allow us to express every aspect of our experience, from joy, faith and praise, to abject misery and profound despair. While more recent songs and hymns are selective and tend to focus on the more positive aspects of life, no human experience was denied or excluded from Israel's worship. As previously mentioned, addressing the psalmists' words to God, making them our own, helps us to articulate feelings which might otherwise be deeply buried or be difficult for us to own.

Using the Psalms to pray seemed acceptable to me, because I was reading Scripture, but I wondered whether other 'set' prayers were legitimate. I was converted in a Baptist Church, where I was greatly helped and grounded in the Christian faith. But there are a few things which subsequently I have had to unlearn, such as the unwritten rule that only extempore (made up on the spot) prayers are the real deal. Actually, many of these spontaneous prayers were very similar to ones prayed on previous weeks, so they were not terribly spontaneous! To use a written prayer was seen as a form of vain repetition. Each prayer had to be freshly prepared, although the effort involved was sometimes challenging and occasionally quite tiring. Using a detailed order of service, a set liturgy, was a sign of dry religiosity, or so I thought. The only prayer we could repeatedly pray was the Lord's Prayer, and even then, I wasn't too sure whether it was legitimate simply to repeat the words, rather than to see each line as a launching pad for certain prayer themes. We could, however, use the words of others to address God in song, which seems somewhat illogical, as hymns are simply sung prayers. The omission of written prayers meant that, unlike in singing, we were denied access to poetic words to express our feelings and desires to God.

Using Set Liturgy

The word 'liturgy' simply means 'the work of the people' and using a written (set) liturgy means that we are praying along with 100s or 1,000s of others around the world. As we form part of a chorus of people who are seeking God's presence, we are participating in an aspect of the communion of saints. These set prayers often balance various facets of prayer, designed to 'cover all the bases' (such as renewing our hope in God, reminding us of the coming kingdom) with prayers of intercession and praise. They can help us to ensure that we don't omit any important areas.

Because they are so wide-ranging, God can use these prayers to bring to mind specific people or situations. *Celtic Daily Prayer* employs the words of Psalm 90:14, 'Oh, satisfy us early with Thy mercy, that we may rejoice and be glad all of our days'. This can prompt us to bring before the Lord situations where material provision, healing or reconciliations is needed, so that in time, we might indeed, actually rejoice. Repeatedly praying those prayers which are direct quotations from Scripture has the added advantage that we memorise sections of the Bible.

Set liturgy is best prayed slowly, leaving silent pauses to allow the Spirit to speak, although if time is short, using it has the advantage that the pace can be changed. Once a set liturgy has been used for some months, much of it can often be recalled from memory, allowing it to be prayed in the car or on public transport. Terry Waite recounts how during his long imprisonment in Lebanon he was sustained each day by praying the Anglican liturgy which he knew by heart.

If, like me, set liturgy is rather alien to your church background, suspend judgment for a time and try it. It is simply a vehicle to help us connect with God and you may come to find it beneficial. Helpful resources include Ffald y Brenin's *Rhythm of Daily Prayer*, *Celtic Daily Prayer* from the Northumbria Community (written and online), as well as the website *Sacred Space*. My approach to prayer has definitely changed over the years. Although I still find it easy to be distracted, it has become easier for me to pray and my definition of prayer has broadened.

All Kinds of Prayer

Early in my Christian life, I assumed prayer meant **intercession.** At the weekly church prayer meeting, we would make our requests known to God, asking him to intervene in people's lives. There were also prayers of adoration and thanksgiving, but mostly it was intercession that came to mind when we talked about prayer. To intercede means to act as an intermediary between two parties, representing one to the other; in this case, we stand between people and God. Intercession is a priestly function and because every believer is a priest, we can all intercede for others (Exodus 19:6). We are all encouraged to pray and trust God for the outcome (James 5:16). If we have a defined role, such as parent or church leader, this carries with it the responsibility to pray for those under our care, but no one's prayer is more or less effective whatever their position might be.

At several points in my life, I have prayed for a list of five to ten people every day for one month, before choosing another group for the subsequent month. I don't tell any of these people that I am praying for them. Some situations that had been stuck for years have shifted during the month when I was praying for them. My prayers are usually quite unsophisticated and generalised, often simply asking that people will be blessed. The focus of prayer for a particular person can change as the month progresses, as I become more attuned to God's will. Perhaps this process is one of the reasons why repeated prayer is necessary.

When we intercede for people God sometimes opens a door of opportunity for us to be the answer to that prayer. I don't mean by this that we should actively create opportunities to do God's work for him - nor should we seek to turn every conversation to God. But when we have been praying, God himself often creates amazing opportunities. We need to learn to recognise when a door has been opened by God and be bold and step through it. I recall praying for a work colleague for nine months when 'out of the blue' he asked me how forgiveness works for Christians - this question had been raised in another a conversation he had had and he thought that I might know the answer. In fact, I had been praying for two people over this same period and they both 'spontaneously' started conversations about God. Perhaps nine months was a symbol of gestation before my prayers gave birth to something. Intercession is an important form of prayer, but it is not the only form.

Praying with the Spirit

A few years after coming to faith I began to speak in tongues. Paul referred to this experience as 'praying with my spirit' - as opposed to praying with our minds (1 Corinthians 14:15). Praying in other languages is a less cerebral form of communication than using our native language and we don't need to stumble to find the right words. I found this was upbuilding, creating a sense of nearness to God and engendering faith, as Paul described in 1 Corinthians 14:2-4. I am sure that there are other ways of praying with our spirit, not limited to those who have been given the gift of praying in tongues. For instance, Paul mentions praying without any words at all, addressing God with 'groans too deep for words' (Romans 8:26).

Christians have differing views on the significance of speaking in tongues, but my experience suggests that not all of those filled with, or baptised in, the Spirit receive this gift. I do wonder, though, whether many more of us would do so if we asked God. One practical approach is to pray every day for a month to receive this gift, avoiding any form of intensity or becoming obsessed with it, but simply being open to the Spirit. If you don't receive the gift you can put the subject to one side and go on your way rejoicing. You have given God an opportunity and he hears all prayer, so it will not have been wasted.

Another form of prayer that relies on our being open to the Spirit is **biblical meditation**. As my definition of prayer was beginning to widen, I discovered this tried and tested way to read Bible stories. The use of imagination in prayer is developed extensively in a series of set meditations developed by Ignatius of Loyola, called *The Spiritual Exercises*. Such approaches involve using our imagination to place ourselves within the story, as on the website *Pray As You Go*. Under the guidance of the Spirit, this sort of biblical meditation can be a very powerful experience, making real the implications of the story for our lives. I usually need to persist as it often takes me 45 minutes before the biblical story begins to connect, while some more practised people may manage this much more quickly.

Allowing God to access our imagination could, in theory, make us more open to bizarre thoughts, yet over many years of leading group biblical meditations, I can only recall people's positive experiences of the presence of God. Perhaps the key element is that the meditation begins with prayer, where we invite the Holy Spirit to speak to us. *The Spiritual Exercises* were, in fact, designed as a handbook for retreat leaders where the person engaging with the series of meditations regularly talks over his or her experience with a retreat guide, as progression is made through the Exercises. Having a trained person to weigh whatever we feel God might have said to us during the meditations acts as an added safeguard.

Speaking Blessing

Shortly after discovering Ignatian prayer, the practice of speaking blessing also came into focus. Blessing was not a new concept to me, as early on in my Christian life I was struck by the power of Jacob's blessing spoken over his sons. He appeared to be prophesying to them, believing that *his own* words would shape the lives of his offspring. Besides which, Paul often ended his letters with a written blessing, to be read aloud to the church: 'The grace of our Lord Jesus Christ be with your spirit' and 'Peace be with you, brothers, and love with faith...' and so on (Galatians 6:18, Ephesians 6:23). Notice that these prayers are not 'Please, Lord, bless the church in Ephesus'. They are examples of direct bold pronouncements spoken to the person concerned and as such are very powerful. I recently heard of someone who repeatedly turned up at the end of an Anglican church service because he so valued hearing the vicar's final words of blessing taken from 2 Corinthians 13:14 - 'And may the grace of the Lord Jesus Christ, the love of God and the fellowship of the Holy Spirit be with you all.'

Blessings are not requests directed to God; they are *addressed to the people* we wish to see benefit, as prophecies are. They are an act of declarative speech, a creative word to that person. This important distinction is made clearer if we adopt the use of the phrase 'speaking blessing', rather than saying we are 'praying for blessing'. I have noticed that sometimes when people begin to speak blessing they easily revert to 'God bless...' prayers. Perhaps it seems more familiar and less risky.

There is a good precedent for this practice. When the disciples were sent on mission they were told to bless the family they stayed with by speaking the words, 'Peace be to this home'. Notice that they were not instructed to intercede for peace - they were told to speak the blessing of peace. Speaking blessing must be important because Jesus instructed them to do this as part of their normal routine (Luke 10:5-6). We bless others as part of our priestly calling and the words themselves are powerful because God's Spirit is behind the words.

There are many ancient blessings we can use, drawn from Scripture or from Celtic liturgy, to enable us to speak powerful blessings over our family, friends, church and neighbourhood. A blessing can break through entrenched situations and bringing a sense of God's presence. We can speak a blessing to people or places with confidence as it conveys God's authority. We still need the sense that God is with us and that his Spirit is prompting us as we speak blessing because this form of prayer is not a magic formula or technique. Here are some examples of blessings which we can speak over people or situations:

NUMBER 6:23-27: The Lord bless you and keep you; The Lord make his face shine on you and be gracious to you; The Lord lift up his countenance upon you and give you peace.

May the peace of the Lord Christ go with you,
wherever he may send you.
May he guide you through the wilderness, protect you through the storm.
May he bring you home rejoicing at the wonders he has shown you.
May he bring you home rejoicing once again into our doors.
CELTIC DAILY PRAYER (MORNING PRAYER)

1 SAMUEL 25:6: Peace to you, and peace be to your house, and peace be to all you have.

2 CORINTHIANS 13:14: The grace of our Lord Jesus Christ and the love of God and the fellowship of the Holy Spirit be with you (all).

May you find peace within the storm,
and the encircling of his arms.
May you find rest within the night, and refreshment in the dawn.
May you find joy within your heart,
a song waiting to be sung.
May you find peace.
© JOHN BIRCH (WWW.FAITHANDWORSHIP.COM)

Creating a Balance in Prayer

In addition to the attentive prayer (contemplation) we looked at in an earlier chapter, we have briefly considered:

- praying through the Psalms

- using set liturgy

- intercession

- praying with our spirit (or *in the Spirit*)

- imaginative meditation on the Bible

- speaking blessing

This is certainly not an exhaustive list and you may find that other approaches to prayer are more conducive. Some people find that singing, or listening to music, is the most natural way for them to enter into God's presence and I would consider these also to be forms of prayer. Others find the best way for them to spend time with God is walking and conversational prayer, as described in David Hansen's aptly named book *Long Wandering Prayer*. Every approach is perfectly legitimate and none is superior to any other.

It would be easy to feel overwhelmed by the sheer variety of the different types of prayer. The main purpose of outlining these different forms of prayer is to help you decide which of these you would like to explore more deeply at this juncture in your life. Perhaps the various forms are more of a menu to choose from, than a 'must-do' list.

Our preferred style of prayer is often a reflection of our personality. It is likely that if we are introverted we might be attracted to silent prayer and to more reflective kinds of prayer. Those of us who are more extraverted may prefer speaking blessing and using singing to aid prayer and so on. Each kind of prayer has its place and we use different kinds of prayer at different times and for different reasons and purposes. It is good to experience them all at some point, even if we are unlikely to find them all equally helpful. We can major on the sort of prayer we find helps us connect most easily with God, very probably using a selection from those listed.

Fasting & Retreat

Fasting and prayer are sometimes mentioned together in Scripture, particularly when there is the need for a spiritual breakthrough or when an important decision needs to be made (Acts 14:23; 13:2-4). Whether fasting should be a regular practice or reserved for certain situations is an issue that is open to debate (there seems more emphasis on fasting in the narrative sections of the Bible than in the Epistles).

Fasting was common Jewish practice in Jesus' day (Matthew 6:16) but it seems as if Jesus did not require his followers to fast routinely. When asked why his disciples did not fast, he replied that there was no need to do so whilst he was present but that, 'The days will come when the bridegroom is taken from them, and then they will fast in that day' (Mark 2:20). Fasting expresses our desire for his presence - we often lose our appetite for food when a loved one is absent. Many of us find fasting difficult, but Jesus did suggest that fasting from food is particularly important when we experience his absence.

I have fasted from food, but I do this quite rarely as I feel ill even if my breakfast is delayed by 10 minutes! If a total fast is too hard, we can always fast, for example, from meat and alcohol, following the example of Daniel chapter 10. Mary Earle, in her book *The Desert Mothers - Practical Spiritual Wisdom for Every Day,* says that in contrast to the continual indulgence of gluttony that is our cultural norm, the Desert Mothers remind us of the virtues of fasting not just from food, but from arrogant and mean-spirited behaviour and conversation, from the need to be in control, frenetic busyness and hurry, to which we might add compulsive shopping and other such addictive behaviours. There is no ready-made set of solutions to these sicknesses of the soul, so we need our equivalent of the desert - time alone to find God - to be made whole.

A retreat, our modern equivalent to the desert, is also a form of fasting because we deny ourselves access to many of the things and people we rely on for our sense of security. This is particularly the case when we have a silent retreat. Learning to rely more on God, our true source of security, is vital for our long-term effectiveness - even Jesus needed a 40-day retreat before commencing his ministry (Luke 4:2). The Spirit led him into the desert because he needed to deal with certain issues. This was the place where he faced (and faced down) those temptations that would inevitably come his way during the next 3 years. He needed to win the spiritual battle *before* he was launched into the next phase of life and ministry. If we embark on a new course too early, before we have won this sort of inner battle, the likelihood is that we will fail.

Practicalities

As someone who has not always found prayer easy, I have a few suggestions based on my own experience. They are pointers for people who want to begin or progress further on the journey of developing a rhythm of prayer.

Suggestion 1: Don't rush at it, start slowly and begin at the shallow end. You could, for instance, read a psalm each morning or evening, and then pray for five minutes based on what you've read. If a verse stands out you could use it as a springboard to pray for whatever situation it brings to mind.

Alternatively, you could use the Lord's Prayer and pause to pray for situations which relate to each phrase. We can make the Lord's Prayer our own by tailoring it to our particular context, asking for what we need, today. For some of us praying for our daily bread is, sadly, a necessity. But even if we feel we have enough to eat, we will likely require other things to meet our material or psychological needs. We can also pray for the needs of others, noting that 'our' in the Lord's prayer is plural, not singular. This implies that we are praying for our community of faith.

Suggestion 2: Wait until you are well established in a morning routine and then add a prayer time at lunchtime or in the evening. Don't worry if you miss one of these times, as it's not a test. Wait until this rhythm feels as natural as brushing your teeth, which might take a couple of months, before adding a third prayer time to your daily rhythm. If you don't have a prayer time at the moment, this progression might sound impossible, but take it slowly and it will develop.

Suggestion 3: Review your prayer pattern every three or four months. You might feel you need to vary your prayer time and spend more time reading the Bible or more time in silence, but don't review your rhythm too frequently or it won't become habitual. You can do this either alone or with someone else, such as a friend, spiritual director or another person whose judgement you trust. A journal can be an encouragement to persist by reminding you of situations which have changed through prayer.

Suggestion 4: Find some good resources to help you. There are lots of helpful online resources as well as books which outline set rhythms of prayer.

Suggestion 5: Include regular times of prayer with others, either face to face, by phone or on the internet.

* * * * *

A blessing, taken from David Cole's book *Celtic Saints: 40 days of devotional readings*:

May you know the joy of walking close with God.
May you know the blessing of maintaining a routine of spiritual fitness.
May the way of life you live be an inspiration to others.

14

Pace

We have already mentioned that natural rhythms are built into creation and that we do well to take account of our need for rhythm in all aspects of our lives. We neglect our need for regular rest, for example, at our peril - our bodies need sleep and the earth needs fallow times. These are times when it seems as if little is happening, but in fact, much is happening beneath the surface.

The rhythm we adopt will be determined by three elements. The first is our personal circumstances, which will dictate certain opportunities and impose particular limitations. The second factor is that our aspirations, what interests or attracts us, will affect the goals we wish to achieve. The third is, of course, God, including his call upon our lives, the doors he opens or closes and the leading of the Spirit. The rhythm we adopt needs to take account of all these factors.

As well as involvement with my family I also highly value my interaction with my local church. Family and church form my base, although, of course, there are sometimes difficulties. One issue that has concerned me over the years, is that I don't feel that I conform to the typical local church leader (I like people but am not very 'pastoral'). In addition, I have various roles which are mainly outside my locality. God has opened several doors, which have surprised me and I have had to rely on the notion that He knows what He is doing! So for much of the time, I am in my study, writing or preparing to speak somewhere (pre-Covid). This means I have periods of intense activity with conferences or meetings and then longer periods of relative solitude, with much less people contact.

This pattern has caused some anxiety, as it seems rather unusual. However, I have found the example of Celtic monasticism particularly helpful in thinking through my own rhythm. Some monks had extended periods of withdrawal before they engaged in public ministry, or would take frequent periods of time out to seek God. Comgall, for example, had a long time of preparation as a hermit before founding the biggest monastic centre in Ireland. Similarly, St Cuthbert is reputed to have been a hermit before taking on the role of the abbot of Lindisfarne. According to David Adam in *Fire of the North*, once he became an abbot he began to realise that his life was too busy. His solution was to withdraw to the remote island of Inner Farne for long periods before re-engaging with the demands of his ministry.

St Columba is another example of this rhythm of withdrawal and engagement. It is difficult to distinguish history from myth, but he is reported to have frequently conversed with angels. On one occasion a blinding light was said to emerge from a hut where he had been praying for an extended period. In similar vein, an Irish monk, Finbarr felt called to live as a hermit on an island in a lough but also had times when people would come to seek his counsel, in much the same way as those who travelled into the Egyptian desert to consult the Desert Mothers and Fathers. These examples reinforce the idea that seeking the presence of God is primary and that we need to find a pattern of engagement and disengagement that enables us to do this.

The lives of these Celtic saints helped me realise that this ancient pattern of engagement and withdrawal is of relevance today, whether we serve God in our families, in 'secular' employ or in a church role. Their monastic rhythm seemed in some way to legitimise the path God appeared to have led me down. I am certainly not comparing myself with these great saints, which would be delusional. I am simply noting that their example was very helpful to me. My times of relative withdrawal often involve a fairly intense study of books on the Bible or Church history. These activities convey to me a deep sense of God, although I realise that I may be unusual in this! This forms the foundation for my having something to contribute in the times of more intensive engagement with others.

Alongside this particular aspect of Celtic monasticism, the rhythm of engagement and withdrawal, there was also an emphasis on having a daily rhythm. This was outlined in a Rule and founded on a regular pattern of prayer.

A Monastic Rhythm

Sometimes, as mentioned, people confuse having a rhythm of prayer with having a rhythm of life, which is more all-encompassing. For example, a retreat centre may have set times of prayer but may be lacking in other necessary aspects of a monastic rhythm. The staff may work hard but find themselves neglecting the need for worship, rest and recreation.

Having a balanced rhythm should, in fact, characterise the communal life of all Christian organisations, as the way in which we live communicates much more than anything we might say. Of course, a retreat centre needs to maintain an income through having guests to stay and looking after and providing for guests involves a great deal of work. Deep down though, there may well be the realisation that if long-term fruitfulness is to be achieved, a manageable pace, often a slower and steadier pace, is needed.

Adopting a distinctive rhythm does not mean that our lives will ever reach a state of perfect balance. I once read a book which advocated a very ordered routine - spending 'quality time' with our families, regularly cleaning our cars, attending to whatever is necessary for our homes, and putting aside enough time for work and worship - a life portioned out in neat packages. This vision (which I found rather scary) seemed to have more to do with the shiny world of some idealised existence than anything resembling my own reality. The desire to develop a rhythm for our lives is not a rod with which to beat ourselves. It is simply a means of naming and prioritising what is important.

A Rule outlines a rhythm for our lives. It functions as a checklist, a handy reminder of the elements of life which are essential to us. It is not a legalistic document and it is no big deal if, for instance, we commit ourselves to have a day off each week but miss it occasionally due to other demands. A Rule helps us have a pattern for our lives which is sustainable in the long term and fit for our onward journey with God.

The Cult of Busyness

A monastic rhythm is a means of personal formation in the way of Christ. It is designed to shape us personally and sculpt our character and relates more to who we are than to our creating an image we may wish to project. It is not at all focused on how we appear to others. Instead, it is concerned with how we appear to ourselves and to God. Our self-image in the monastic tradition is very different from how we evaluate ourselves in many contemporary societies. We tend to put a high value on having a good job, on being productive, influential or 'useful', and we have even come to define ourselves in terms of our role in society, 'what we do'. We can easily over-invest time, resources and emotional energy into maintaining our social standing and become enslaved to the cult of busyness.

Busy-ness can become the key to our feeling significant and being a *busy* parent, a *busy* carer or a *busy* teacher etc., is often viewed as being desirable. We may well feel rather smug if we can sustain this high level of activity, but it is likely that we will also feel stressed - and that we will become difficult to live with as a result. One of the benefits of adopting a monastic rhythm is that it legitimises certain activities that are important for our long-term well-being, but which are not to do with 'getting things done'. As a friend in the church once said, 'We are human beings, not human doings'.

A Rule prioritises aspects of life that we might consider less urgent or important in the onward rush to achieve. Clearly, there are practical constraints on our time and our personal circumstances may leave us with little choice as to how to order our lives. But even if our circumstances are limiting, a Rule can prompt and guide us to think creatively about how we might carve out time for areas of life which are all too easily neglected.

The equation *busyness* = *worthiness* is also prevalent in the Church. Regrettably, the words 'busy' and 'pastor' seem to go together quite naturally, as the insightful author Eugene Peterson has pointed out. Being too active is often considered praiseworthy, but it produces an intensity that is unattractive. It is also counterproductive. When people follow our example they are likely to end up with equally unappealing lives. We do want to be wholly committed to God and we are sometimes busy out of necessity, but it is very easy to put pressure on ourselves (and others) by confusing overactivity with spirituality.

We tend to feel sorry for Martha in the story told by Luke and we can identify with her busy preparations in honour of Jesus (10:40). The fact that this story is so memorable suggests that her life reflects the lives of so many of us who, similarly, seek to honour Jesus. Intensity, always being in a rush, rarely communicates a sense of God's presence to others.

I recall someone telling me that he had stayed with the pastor of a large church and that there was a Bible in the bathroom, implying that he was so busy that this might be his only opportunity to read Scripture! My friend was impressed by this but to me, it seemed a symptom of a Christian culture whose values simply reflect those of the surrounding society. This situation requires urgent readjustment and adopting a monastic rhythm might be the solution.

Work & Worship

The four terms *work, worship, rest and recreation* act as a framework to rethink the balance of our lives. I am sure that these terms have been used before and that I have come across them in my reading, but I cannot recall where! These activities are not always clear cut and distinct from one another, but having such a framework helps us create a well-balanced rhythm for our lives.

The first two components of a monastic rhythm are work and worship. Work often has financial or other rewards, including the feeling that we are contributing to the common good. It can be a way in which we express our creativity or employ our gifts and abilities. But work is still a completely legitimate involvement when it is less personally rewarding and is simply a way of earning a living.

Work refers to any effort we make to be productive or useful. Being an unpaid homemaker, a carer, volunteering or helping others is just as much work as having a paid role. Even when we are 'retired' we still engage in work - I prefer the phrase 'achieving financial independence', as we never retire from seeking to serve God in whatever way we are able.

Worship acts as a counterbalance to work, reminding us that God created us and sustains us. His active presence is the rock on which our creativity and our efforts to earn a living ultimately depend. Worship reminds us that we are not fully in control of our destiny. In a parable, Jesus describes an industrious farmer who believed he was fully in control of the future. Being hardworking and successful, he was someone whom we might regard as a model citizen. He was making wise plans for the future, prudently building a new barn for his large harvest of crops. It could appear harsh that he was described as a fool, but that is what he was, for that very night he was to die and appear before his maker - his 'soul would be required of him'. It seems that he trusted in his possessions rather than in God and was for all practical purposes an atheist, depending entirely on his own abilities (Luke 12:20).

When we are successful in work we can easily place ourselves at the centre of our universe and think that our destiny is entirely in our own hands, rather like the farmer in the parable. This belief is a delusion, a form of disorientation. The cure is worship as it reorientates us by placing God back in the centre. Worship dethrones self and enthrones God, helping us to once more orientate ourselves to reality. When we pray *'Give us this day our daily bread',* it is a healthy reminder to us in the West that we are ultimately dependent on God's provision and that we're asking God to provide whatever we need.

Rest

For different people rest takes different forms, such as a walk in the countryside, watching a favourite film, or reading a novel. It also encompasses those times when we simply put our lives on pause. Rest is important as it provides time for review and celebration. We read in Genesis that when God had created the universe he rested, sat back, coffee in hand and looked admiringly at the work that he had done (ok - the coffee bit was made up). He took time to enjoy it, to rejoice, to celebrate and this is a good example to follow. Rest provides the opportunity to mull over the last week and review what has been achieved.

Rest was built into the fabric of Old Testament faith - even the fields in ancient Israel were allotted periods of rest, fallow times when the land could recover. Situations in which we have no time to rest, where we are expected to be continually productive, resonate with that of the Children of Israel enslaved in Egypt. Following their escape, the Sabbath was instigated to act as a reminder to Israel that they were no longer slaves.

Sabbath also enshrined the importance of rest for Israel in another way: it provided a regular time to look back and recall what God had done for them. They were reminded of the history of their national deliverance in order to enable them to rest in God's redemptive work. When we fail to look back at what God has done we end up living in the moment. We develop amnesia and become spiritually disorientated, forgetting our history with God.

It is beyond the scope of this book to look at the relationship between Sunday and the Jewish Sabbath, but one important point is relevant to the topic of rest: Sunday worship needs to provide an opportunity to look back and celebrate what God has done, primarily in the Cross and the Resurrection. Sometimes church services are overly filled with content or used as opportunities to communicate the vision for certain projects to rally the troops, in which case we are unlikely to benefit from the potential for 'Sabbath rest'.

One reason why Communion, the Lord's Supper, is so important is that it looks back to what God had done and re-grounds us in our history as his people (as well as helping us to look forward in faith). Hymns and songs also help us to do this. Testimony is another effective way to celebrate what God has done more recently; it is also an opportunity to pass on our experience of the faithfulness of God from one generation to another (Psalm 145:4). This works both ways: it is hugely encouraging when the younger generation pass on their current experience of God to those of us who are older.

Recreation

Rest and recreation are easily confused with each other, but they are worth differentiating as they each serve a different purpose. Recreation differs from rest in that it is more active - it implies engaging in activities which *re-create* us. Physical exercise, for example, will actually recreate us physically, turning fat into muscle, while walking in beautiful surroundings will rejuvenate and restore our soul. Some aspects of our devotional life will re-create us, renewing our sense of God's presence in our lives. When we do something as simple as listening to our favourite spiritual song and perhaps sing along it re-creates us inwardly, refreshing and renewing us spiritually. Re-creation restores vitality and renews our strength.

We need to build recreation into our lives and my wife and I do this by having a day off each week. We may go out for a walk, or to a film in the winter, or we potter indoors, avoiding any activity that feels like a chore, avoiding anything in fact that we feel we *have* to do. We talk together but try to avoid looking at emails. We try not to be too serious and ensure that if we talk about work or church, we look at its personal impact rather than having a business meeting. This practice does renew us.

The first book I read on the monastic life had the words *the love of learning* in its title. One aspect of recreation is the practice of learning new things. We are now aware that learning a new language or learning to play a musical instrument, for example, helps protect us against developing dementia. New neural pathways are created as we acquire new knowledge or learn new skills, and new horizons are opened to us. Learning is wider than academic study - it includes acquiring any new skill, such as knitting or hedge laying. I recently did my first ever woodwork project (since my dismal attempts at school), building a cabinet for a speaker. I enjoyed it so much that I was sad when I had finished it.

Whenever I talk to groups about work, worship, rest and recreation people point out that there is an overlap between these activities. That's true, but distinguishing between them can be helpful because we need all four components to ensure that we are equipped to face life. Specific activities often straddle two or more of these categories. For example, I like music and when I listen to my favourite CD I am enjoying rest; but when I am playing my guitar at home and learning new scales, that is recreation. If, on the other hand, I am rehearsing to play live music at a gig that comes under the category of work. This might sound pedantic but it is useful to distinguish these aspects because too much rehearsing (work) means that I get little recreational value out of my playing.

An Inventory

It can be helpful to use the idea of a monastic rhythm as a form of inventory, to evaluate our current patterns of living, before going on to consider what a modern-day Rule might look like. This will help us to see the particular areas we might need to address.

Perhaps you can map your day, week and year and see how much time is given to each of these components. Alternatively, you could simply list the different ways in which you engage with work, worship, rest and recreation. You can ask yourself questions such as: which tasks do I undertake to produce something functional (work)? How do I build in rest and for how much time? This can help you see whether the balance seems right and where you might want to make adjustments.

A suitable Rule for today will include a balance of work and worship, rest and recreation because together these components enable us to be fully human. The story of Creation indicates that we are designed to live with these factors in balance. The first human beings were placed in a garden to care for and work the land; they were to be generative and give rise to other humans; they experienced creativity, for instance, by choosing names for the animals. They also enjoyed the presence of God in the cool of the evening, experiencing the rest which results from the friendship of the Lord.

15

Practicalities

None of us knows the future.
None of us knows when we will meet sudden darkness in our lives.
None of us knows the moment when the most essential thing will be
that the lamps of our faith be well supplied with oil so that we can
show the light of Christ to those around us and to those who love us.
To be able to do that is not a matter of a moment's impulsive courage.
It is a matter of a person's life-long character. It is the outcome of a
life well-lived in love and prayer.
PAUL O'REILLY SJ (HOPE IN ALL THINGS)

This book is based on the idea that a Rule of Life is the heart of anything
we might label 'New Monasticism'. As we have seen, New Monasticism
is the quest to develop an integrated spiritual life based on repurposing
ancient monastic practices and our particular focus has been on Celtic
Christianity. We have now come to the point where we can draw together
many of the previously considered elements to form a Rule.

**You might want to skip this chapter if you already have a Rule
of Life - or if you are not interested in developing one at this
juncture.**

To summarise what we have previously looked at:

- The motivation to adopt a Rule is a desire for deeper communion with God. It is a way to experience God's presence *with us* - and to develop practices that enable others to experience his presence *through us*.

- A Rule is also a practical expression of discipleship. It helps us follow in the footsteps of Jesus. The aim is not to earn God's favour but to find practical ways to 'walk humbly with your God' (Micah 6:8).

- A Rule consists of what we have described as a monastic rhythm. Such rhythms need to be sustainable and tailored to our individual circumstances and personalities.

- Prayer is foundational to any Rule. How we outwork a rhythm of prayer has to take account of the competing demands on our time and the needs of those around us.

With these points in mind, we are in a position to consider the shape of a contemporary New Monastic Rule. The following is simply one example of what a Rule for today might look like and it is not intended to be prescriptive. It is a broad outline of the practices we might include; these can be adopted or adapted, with specific details to be worked out according to our own context. It aims to be practical rather than to describe a set of values or aspirations and, therefore, it is expressed as a series of commitments to action - it contains a degree of challenge in order that we might grow.

A Rule for Today

A Rule inspired by Celtic Christianity will encompass the topics we have covered so far - prayer, pilgrimage, possessions, pride, people, proximity, places and pace. Using Celtic and other forms of monasticism as our guide means that we approach the practicalities of a Rule inspired by their example. However, inspiration alone will not create the conditions for personal transformation, so we need to find ways to earth these different areas practically. In order to make the shape of our Rule more understandable we can group our chapter titles under three main headings with respect to how they relate to:

GOD

COMMUNITY

SELF

These three headings recall the Old Testament commandments which Jesus famously prioritised: loving **God** and loving our **neighbour** as we love **ourselves** (Matthew 22:36-40). These two greatest commandments, as we have seen, are a concise summary of how to live, akin to a Rule of Life.

The practices which relate to **GOD** include **prayer** and **pilgrimage**. Prayer creates the right conditions to make us more finely attuned to God's presence, especially when our posture in prayer is one of attentiveness. Prayer can also involve biblical meditation, which is a way of listening carefully for God's still small voice mediated through Scripture. It also includes intercession and speaking blessing - ways in which we aim to cultivate God's tangible presence in our own and others' lives.

Pilgrimage in the Celtic tradition relates to an awareness that we are called to carry God's presence with us wherever we go, whether at home or abroad. It relies on our listening for the voice of the Spirit combined with a willingness to allow him to set our agenda. Pilgrimage also recognises that God is the prime mover in mission; we are invited to follow his lead and join him in whatever he is doing.

COMMUNITY refers to those topics we have considered in the chapters on **people**, **proximity** and **places**. We reflect God's grace when we are hospitable and when we seek to develop genuine friendship. In this way we mirror the way in which Jesus related to others and we embody the heart of the Gospel, which is that God has welcomed us with open arms.

God is attentive to us as individuals but he is also concerned with our communities and the places where we find ourselves living or working. Alongside pilgrimage, a distinctive emphasis in Celtic Christianity is the awareness that our community or our home might become a thin place, where God's presence is easily experienced. This is only likely to become a reality when we are committed to a particular place and actively embrace God's call to become firmly rooted in a community.

SELF encompasses the practices examined in the chapters on **pride** and **pace**. It has been suggested that the monastic emphasis on obedience relates to humility, which was regarded as the antidote to pride. For us, this involves openness, accountability and the sort of humility that recognises that we are not the final arbiters of truth, nor the font of all wisdom. Pace is about creating a sustainable rhythm for our lives. We can develop routines that ensure that we balance work and worship, have rest and find ways to be re-created physically, psychologically and spiritually.

I have also included the topic of **possessions** under the heading of SELF. This is because the monastic vow of poverty relates to our becoming free from other distractions and attachments in order to fully pursue God's presence. Although generosity (involving time, money and employing our gifts) certainly helps others, it also has a profoundly positive effect on the one who is being generous.

A New Monastic Rule

Based on the chapter titles and the three headings God, Community and Self a New Monastic Rule might look like this:

GOD

1. I will develop a rhythm of prayer and Bible reading (**Prayer**).

2. I will seek to hear God's voice, to discern his activity and join him in his mission of love to the world (**Pilgrimage**).

COMMUNITY

3. I will aim to be hospitable to others and to develop genuine friendships both within and outside the Church (**People & Proximity**).

4. I will be rooted in my local community and seek to cultivate God's presence where I live and work (**Places**).

SELF

5. I aim to be open with others and will find contexts for personal accountability (**Pride**).

6. I will develop a good rhythm of work, worship, rest and recreation (**Pace**).

7. I will be generous with my time, money and gifts so that I give up what I cannot keep in order to gain what I cannot lose (**Possessions**).

(The last phrase in section 7 paraphrases Jim Elliot's famous quote).

* * * * *

We have seen that monastic Rules are often summed up in a phrase to act as a reminder of the main themes characterising each religious order. This helps monks and nuns focus their attention on the core issues for their order and to frame their practices in that context. Franciscans, who refer to themselves as brothers rather than monks, summarise their manner of life in the phrase *poverty, chastity and obedience.* Benedictine monks and nuns subscribe to the trinity of *stability, obedience and continual conversion.* These particular vows are then outworked in a set of detailed practices which together constitute a monastic rhythm of work, worship, rest and recreation. A possible aide-memoire for a New Monastic Rule could be a combination of some of the chapter headings in part three; for example, *prayerful attentiveness, proximity and pilgrimage* - or you could choose other terms appropriate to your calling.

Contextualising a Rule

A Rule is a practical guide to everyday living, and inevitably, this will be expressed differently in different contexts. Someone who is a full-time carer for elderly relatives will outwork a Rule in a different way than a student or a nurse would because there are different opportunities and constraints involved in each occupation. How might we tailor a Rule to an individual's circumstances? The best approach is to work on it gradually. The different components of the Rule will not all be addressed at the same time.

Someone might decide that they need to start with developing a rhythm of prayer. Many of us find that prayer can easily be relegated to near the bottom of our list of priorities, so this is a good place to start. In this case, you could initially focus on having a time of prayer in the morning. Once this is well established it is possible to add an evening prayer time and much later to include prayer at lunchtime.

Once this is properly underway a different area can be addressed, such as the need to establish a good rhythm of life, with adequate rest and recreation. If you find you tend to work too much a good start would be to have a half-day off each week, perhaps spending time exploring your local area.

The gradual process of working through the implications of a Rule might take a year or more. Trying to do too much too soon is likely to result in feeling overwhelmed. There is great value in working out the practicalities with others, such as a close friend, spiritual director or partner, drawing on their wisdom and providing an opportunity to share your progress.

The Rule for Leaders

For those of us in leadership roles, both in the church and wider society, there are factors to take into account when applying a Rule to our lives. The dynamics of leadership can be challenging and no one makes perfect strategic decisions all the time. Expectations can be high, however, and in the face of repeated scrutiny, the comments of others, even when they are simply neutral observations, can feel persecutory. If we feel that we are continually being judged, it can lead to depression and a high proportion of leaders report that this is the case. Alternatively, it can create defensiveness or lead to our becoming arrogant and overly self-assured. In either case, a guarded, insular, stance easily develops over time. With this in mind, it is worth thinking through how these pressures on a leader might affect the outworking of a Rule.

Because of these dynamics, leaders who start with good motives can become susceptible or vulnerable to various enticements, often involving money, sex or power. Falling prey to failings in such areas requires that, if they are not already in place, developing accountability structures is a priority in outworking a Rule, where there can be openness and honesty. This is not always easy - choosing who to involve in an accountability forum needs careful thought. Sharing our weaknesses, thoughts and feelings in a manner that is too indiscriminate can backfire and draw criticism. One possibility is to seek out someone who is separate from immediate ministry contexts, such as a spiritual director, or mentor. Since these are people who have no personal investment in the leader's life, it is easier for the leader in question to be honest about doubts, fears or failings.

It is not always straightforward to build community on an equal footing with those who look to us for leadership. A significant minority of people carry an inbuilt difficulty with authority figures, often due to past experiences, and are liable to challenge people in leadership roles at any opportunity; others do the opposite and put leaders on a pedestal, falsely believing that they can do no wrong. When these sorts of reactions occur it is difficult for those in leadership to build genuine community. A leader might need to seek to build community by seeking to have a few close friends who treat him or her as they would anyone else - friends who are prepared to provide both support and challenge.

If the whole leadership team of a church or organisation embrace a Rule, they might have a rhythm of prayer together twice weekly - or members of the leadership team could adopt the same liturgy to use in their own homes. Humility would involve an agreement to be open about thoughts and feelings in team meetings. This would require the team to agree that openness does not mean that others are constrained to agree with any strongly expressed opinions and to realise that diversity of approach is to be expected.

Creating Sustainable Patterns of Living

If you want your dream to be
Take your time, go slowly
Do few things but do them well
Heartfelt work grows purely.
DONOVAN LEITCH (LITTLE CHURCH)

It will be evident that embracing a Rule is a very different approach from trying out certain spiritual disciplines for a limited length of time such as, for example, a month of 'radical discipleship'. The pattern embodied in a Rule aims to continually refocus our lives on God, and, when it is employed over many years, it grounds us in his presence.

We noted earlier that Benedict's Rule aimed to counter extreme practices and to curb any tendency we might have towards perfectionism. Being 'good enough' is, as it says, good enough, even if it means that we are quite modest in our initial aims. Sustainability is more important than having very challenging goals which may turn out to be unattainable.

It might be practical, for instance, for our daily rhythm to involve our reading a psalm and quietly praying as we travel to and from work on the train. A weekly rhythm might include a day when we put aside work, emails and social obligations to create a space for rest and/or recreation. We could build in regular opportunities for hospitality as part of our monthly routine. Our annual rhythm might include attending a conference or going on a retreat.

Having an achievable Rule helps us avoid being overly zealous, something which can be unattractive to others. We do not need to prove ourselves worthy - our goal is to love God and our neighbour and to cultivate God's presence, not to demonstrate how well we can do.

16

Perseverance

Finding the Right Path

Many of the paths we choose in life are not, in fact, unique to us - they are well-worn paths which have been trodden before us. We become aware of what seems to be the right path, but the destination is not always clear when we first set out. We may recognise the next step we should take but often have to trust that God knows the overall direction. Abraham, the father of faith, is our example to follow. He was clear in his spirit that he had to set out but he 'went out, not knowing where he was going' (Hebrews 11:8).

There are similar stories of Celtic monks who set out in boats, trusting that the winds and tides would take them wherever God wanted them to end up. We might regard them as somewhat naïve today, but, on the other hand, we are unlikely to set out at all if we require too much information about the destination before we move. We might wish that God's guidance resembled a map which lays out the whole route before we begin the journey, but it is usually more like a Satnav, directing which way to turn just before we reach a junction.

Looking back at my journey I can identify certain points at which I chose a particular path (or perhaps I simply identified the path chosen for me). Having been in church leadership for many years, the decision to study at a theological college was an important path that took an unexpected turn. Although I was keen to study biblical interpretation, it was the stories and sayings of the Desert Fathers and of Ignatius Loyola which had a more lasting impact. I was particularly attracted to Ignatian spirituality, with its emphasis on discerning God's will, engaging in mission and its deep roots in the Bible. I believe that deep down I had been looking for something along these lines and that this had been an unconscious quest, more of an inner restlessness than something I could clearly identify beforehand. Another significant journey began when I encountered Celtic Christianity. We visited Ffald y Brenin retreat centre in the 1990s, a set of converted farm buildings, situated beneath a mountain in West Wales. Its name means 'Sheepfold of the King' in Welsh. St Brynach, a Celtic Christian, had prayed in a cell situated near the site where the centre now stands. Many people reported having seen angels on the hill behind the monk's cell as he prayed, so this location became known as *Carningli*, 'the mount of angels'. There is a mysterious dynamic between people and place such that, as in the example of St Brynach and Carningli, the ongoing and continual presence of a person of prayer cultivates God's enduring presence in that place. Over 40 years ago a couple, Peter and Phyllida Mould, purchased the farmhouse at Ffald y Brenin to refurbish it as a retreat centre subsequently established a rhythm of prayer, something which has continued to be foundational.

During one of our retreats there, my wife purchased a book on Celtic spirituality and said that I should read it. I declined, saying that I had explored spirituality enough for now and needed to work through what I had already learned. But she persisted, reminding me that I had been given a prophecy to the effect that I would need to be prepared to go around a well-trodden path despite my reluctance to do so. So I capitulated! Reading about the Celtic monks and experiencing Ffald y Brenin as 'a thin place' led me down the path outlined in this book.

But these high points in the journey are only part of the story, as life has not always been easy since that time. Eugene Peterson, the author of *The Message*, uses a wonderful phrase, *the mystery and the mess,* to describe our experience of God and of life. Life can feel like a mess, whether that is due to Covid-19, political upheaval or our own personal circumstances. But in the midst of the mess, we can still experience the mystery of the presence of God - particularly when we seek to cultivate his presence. My commitment to a Rule was stimulated by reading a chapter in David Runcorn's *A Spirituality Handbook* and this helped me find mystery in the mess.

Persistence

Let us press on to know the LORD; his going out is sure as the dawn; he will come to us as the showers, as the spring rains that water the earth.
HOSEA 6:3

It can sound very cliched to suggest, as I have done, that life is a journey, but that is what it is. There are high points and low points on our journey, but the important thing is that we continue to press on despite the temptation to give up. Seeking to know more of God's presence is all the more important when we face pressures and challenges. It is important that we acknowledge the actual realities of our lives at these times.

Some suggest that if we are faithful to God then all will go well in life. There is a partial truth in this view, as God often blesses us when we seek him, but, as Job found out, this is not always immediate. Faith exercised in adversity is highly valued by God, but it does not always guarantee what we might consider to be successful outcome. The writer to the Hebrews mentions some whose faith had a less than desirable outcome - they 'were sawn in two... destitute, afflicted, mistreated...' These are included alongside Abraham, Moses and Enoch (Hebrews 11:37). In fact, faith is often seen most clearly in suffering and the theme of perseverance amid difficulties and times of testing is to be found everywhere in Scripture.

It is difficult to hang on to a sense of hope when we are physically, emotionally or spiritually drained, even when we are aware that God's presence is promised. Aragorn's words in Tolkien's allegory *The Lord of the Rings* sums up the sort of perseverance we need in our Christian journey: 'With hope or without hope we will follow the train of our enemies'. Perhaps we could reword this: 'With hope or without hope we will pursue the presence of God'. To admit that we sometimes lack hope can sound as if we are saying that we lack faith, but faith is less a feeling and more of an active trust. It is about keeping going when our experience mirrors that of Paul when he wrote: 'we were so utterly burdened beyond our strength that we despaired of life itself' (2 Corinthians 1:8).

An approach to spirituality that is genuinely Christian involves a determination to persist whatever our external circumstances or internal moods. An alternative is to retreat into triumphalism, which is the fanciful creation of a bubble world where we insist that all is well, despite the fact it clearly isn't. Triumphalism looks to the victory of God on the Cross but ignores the fact that we too are called to take up our cross. Realism about the journey recognises that along the way we will both encounter difficulties and have success.

A Rule can help us when we find ourselves in difficult circumstances. Several of the practices we have looked at can encourage us and help us to persist. Scripture-based prayers renew our hope and trust. Regularly reading the Psalms reminds us of the ups and downs of God's people through the ages and how God acts on their behalf. We can suffer from spiritual amnesia when we go through challenging times and forget that God does hear us. The American theologian Walter Brueggemann is helpful here. He pointed out that the Psalms often relate a pattern of orientation (all is well), disorientation (when things go wrong) followed by reorientation when God has acted externally or changed us internally. The last phase, reorientation, signals that we have forged a real-world faith and emerged stronger from our trials.

Involvement in our Christian community, as part of a Rule, is also helpful in times of trial. It makes support and encouragement a possibility as we remain connected to others when our natural tendency might be to withdraw. A Rule also ensures that we continue with regular prayer and other practices, irrespective of whether we are on the mountaintop or in the valley. Prayer places us in the context where we can experience the presence of God afresh and be renewed. Faith and patience eventually pay off and if we persevere we will make progress as dawn inevitably follows the darkness (Hebrews 6:12). If we keep a journal then reading it when life is bleak is a helpful reminder of this dynamic.

Bread for the Journey & a Sword for the Fight

The Lord of the Rings is the story of a difficult journey, an allegory of the cosmic struggle which is the backdrop to the Christian life. There is a similar story in 1 Samuel 21, where David is on the run, pursued by Saul's warriors. Life had taken an unexpected turn for the worse, despite Samuel's assurance that he was God's chosen king. David was experiencing the mess, rather than the mystery at this point! He came to a shrine and rather audaciously ate the 'holy' bread, which had been dedicated to the Lord. In addition to food, he needed a weapon and was given the sword of Goliath, whom he had previously slain.

In his book *Leap Over a Wall* Peterson uses a memorable phrase to describe this story, suggesting that David was given *bread for the journey and a sword for the fight*. We also need these same two things. We acquire 'bread' through those practices in a Rule which strengthen us: prayer, reading the Bible, cultivating friendship, and encountering God in times of solitude. A 'sword' includes prayer but it also reminds us of what Paul refers to as *the whole armour of God* (Ephesians 6:10-20). This involves attitudes and practices which shape the way we live. The powerful effect of a righteousness life is emphasised by Jesus when he stated that Satan has 'nothing in me' (John 14:30). A Rule enables us to live for others, in keeping with the Gospel, avoiding pride and selfishness. These attitudes and practices are particularly important in times of suffering when we might easily turn inwards or give up.

In recent years I have been involved with a series of conferences which bring together leaders in the Catholic Charismatic Renewal and those from the New Charismatic Churches (formerly referred to as 'non-denominationals'). These conferences have been a wonderfully instructive experience and no more so than when the theme one year was suffering and blessing. Within my circles (New Charismatic) the emphasis is often on blessing and triumph over adversity, whereas the Catholic Church has often emphasised the place of suffering in the life of the Church. Of course, these two dimensions of our experience dovetail with one another, but even those of us who experience many blessings will inevitably face many difficulties, disappointments and bereavement, and it is noteworthy that persecution of Christians is currently at the highest level recorded in the history of the Church. Experiences of suffering are inevitable and it is important to think how suffering and God's presence might be linked.

God's Presence & Suffering

Yours is the day, yours also the night...
PSALM 74:16

The subject of this book, *Cultivating God's Presence,* would be incomplete without looking at the place of suffering. Many of the stories of God's presence are remarkable and describe incredibly positive and uplifting experiences. But we all have times of desperation and times when we feel abandoned by God, sometimes for considerable periods. While there have been those who have romanticised Celtic Christianity, we know that the life of a pilgrim monk was not an easy one, embracing many challenges, including exposure to physical danger. The stories which come down to us naturally recount triumphs over adversity, but there must have also been many whose experience was less positive and whose journeys resulted in little obvious success.

Sometimes Christians, particularly those in the West, associate God's presence with blessing and when they experience suffering, find it presents a huge challenge to their belief system. During my student days, I attended a Pentecostal church, where I learnt much about the moving of the Holy Spirit. The sermon that made the most impact on me was not, however, focused on healing or other gifts. It was a talk by a missionary who had returned from Latin America with a chronic illness, which had cut short his ministry there. His continued trust in God despite his experience was evident. He was a living example of faith in adversity.

The book of Job is an extended reflection on the experience and the meaning of suffering. It is probably the oldest book in the Old Testament and the central character is identified as a God-fearing sheikh, but not necessarily an Israelite. One commentator suggested that the central feature of the book is the question Satan implies. He asks God, in effect, 'do you really think Job would worship you if it were not for all the benefits you give him?' (Job 1:9-11). This frames Job's suffering as a test to see if we follow God even when the cost seems to outweigh the benefits. This does not necessarily imply that God sets up trials, but it points to the fact that we live in a fallen world, where there is spiritual opposition to God's people. Job's response tests his motivation; is it the love of God which constrains us to live rightly or is it the love of self? One commentator expressed this along the lines of, 'Is there such a thing on earth as a disinterested following of God?' Job's life, as well as the lives of the Celtic pilgrim monks, suggests that there can be a positive answer to this question. The final words of the well-known prayer of Teresa of Avila seem relevant to the story of Job: 'Let nothing disturb you. Let nothing frighten you. All things are passing. God is unchanging.' Her prayer continues, 'patient endurance attains to all things', concluding with the words, 'Whoever has God, lacks nothing. God alone suffices'. It is also reminiscent of Paul's encouragement to persevere, 'the God of peace **will** soon crush Satan under your feet' (Romans 16:20).

Holy Agnosticism

Agnosticism has two meanings. The first, and most common, is when people affirm that God is unknowable. The word comes from the Greek for knowledge (gnosis) and the prefix - a - which means not. In this view, which is not an orthodox Christian view, we can neither affirm nor deny God's existence. The second meaning of agnosticism, less commonly used, relates to the belief that we can say certain things about God but that it is futile to try to seek to understand God in ways which leave no room for mystery. We can have certainty about the fact that, for instance, God loves us, Jesus is divine and yet came to earth in human form and so on. But we cannot finally explain why a particular person experiences hardships or suffering. We are unable to explain it beyond pointing to the mystery which characterises not only God himself but also his ways and thoughts. I suggest that this view which allows for such mystery and can be referred to as *holy agnosticism* is more likely to help us persevere when the going is tough than trying to come up with an explanation for our circumstances.

Job's comforters were, however, more certain, believing that prosperity inevitably follows our faithfulness to God and that suffering is a sign of God's disfavour. In Job's case, in fact, the exact opposite was true - he was singled out by Satan purely because he was so righteous and was described by God as being 'blameless' (Job 1:8). In 2006 I taught an Old Testament course at a Bible College in the rural Eastern Cape, South Africa. We spent a whole day on Job and I was aware that many of the pastors present had experienced vastly more suffering than I ever had. As we concluded, one young man, who had been shot and nearly killed in an armed hold-up, was in tears. The thing which had moved him so much was that God never explained to Job why he had suffered. Even at the end of the book, Job was still in the dark about Satan's challenge, which formed the backdrop to his hardships. Just like this young man, Job never got to know the answer to the question, 'Why me?'

Whenever we ask, 'Why me?' we can end up blaming ourselves, or we blame God for letting us down. It has been said that a better question to ask ourselves might be, 'Why *not* me?' especially as Christianity has suffering at its very heart, with the Cross as its universal symbol, and encompasses a well-thought-out theology of suffering.

Holy agnosticism saves us from speculation as we direct our mental energy towards facing whatever confronts us. Our natural response to adversity should, of course, be to pray for deliverance from whatever or whoever is causing us to experience hardship. But there are times when we pray and despite our faith, God doesn't remove our 'thorn in the flesh' (1 Corinthians 12:7). We don't know the precise nature of Paul's thorn, but we know that suffering comes our way in many guises - illness, family pressures, isolation, psychological trauma, the loss of home or livelihood, as well as through prejudice or persecution.

We pray that God the Father would deliver us from evil and sometimes God *does* deliver us from suffering in response to prayer (Psalm 103:1-3). When people are healed our faith is built up, and, conversely, when our prayers are seemingly unanswered, our faith can be battered. But it is important to recognise that whether we are healed or continue to suffer we are exercising the same faith in each case. As if to emphasise this point, on two occasions the writer to the Hebrews commended the faith of those who persisted even though, as yet, they had 'not received what is promised' (Hebrews 11:13 and 39).

The Apostle Paul had opponents who claimed that his sufferings were a sign that he was 'all talk' and that he actually lacked spiritual authority. In his most personal and self-revealing writing, Paul describes his suffering in detail and turns his enemies' arguments to his advantage. He suggests that his personal history confirms that he is a genuine apostle because apostleship involves suffering (2 Corinthians 11 and 12). A Christian response to suffering is not to deny its reality or seek to be untouched by it. This is, in fact, the approach that Buddhism promotes and the aim is to regard it as irrelevant to our current existence. In contrast, Christians join with the pain of all creation, longing for something better. It is our hope of God's future action which makes all the difference (Romans 8:22-29).

Suffering & Glory

Theologians explore the theme of suffering under the title of 'theodicy' - this is a compound term linking together the Greek for 'God' and 'justify'. How can we, in effect, justify God in the face of so much suffering? This is beyond the scope of this book, apart from the affirmation already made that suffering is often a mystery and also to affirm that there is a relationship between suffering and God's presence, His glory. The following stories illustrate different aspects of this.

I started my working life as a medical doctor. I was in family medicine for several years and I remember an elderly couple who were my patients. They were faithful Christians and I had to visit them regularly. As well as their physical suffering, which made life difficult for them, they had both had terrible childhoods, having been badly mistreated in orphanages. This experience left them with enduring mental scars. I realised that there was very little I could do for them medically but they appreciated the contact. I found these visits a positive and uplifting experience. This lovely couple made me think a lot about the relationship between healing and suffering. This was back in the 1980s when there was a big emphasis on the healing ministry. For one thing, I realised that they were not following God out of self-interest, because God had not stopped their pain, despite, I imagine, their having called out to him to do so. They were faithful people who believed that behind it all, despite any evidence to the contrary, there was a Father who loved them. Their home was a place where I experienced the presence of God.

Much more recently I received an email from somebody whom I met a year ago. He comes from a long line of Christian ministers and now has a full-time role in helping start churches in different parts of the world. We spoke at the same conference, but he had to leave before I spoke as he was experiencing intense physical pain, as a result of a longstanding medical condition. When in severe pain he can only rest. In my email conversation with him, I asked him how he was getting on since we had met. He said that there had been no change in his condition but added that through the pain he had experienced much good and, to use his words, much 'glory'.

The third story was told to me by a friend who is a leader in a large

Chinese church network. He had witnessed the meeting of a Chinese pastor, who had been imprisoned for over 20 years, with a Christian author from the USA. She had asked this elderly pastor what had led to his imprisonment and was told that there had been a book written many years before, suggesting that many of the Chinese churches were cults. The content of the book had been used by the Chinese authorities as an excuse to imprison him. The author realised to her horror that it was *her* book which had led to his incarceration. She apologised profusely for the unintended part she had played in causing his suffering, bitterly regretting what she had written. After the book had been published she had realised that her information was factually incorrect, and had subsequently retracted her views, but tragically that had all been too late for the pastor. He had missed his children growing up and had been subject to extreme privation and torture, yet his response to the visiting author's profuse apology was quite unexpected. He told her that he would not change the past at all. He had experienced the presence of God so much more in his imprisonment than he had done previously and he regarded it as a blessing.

The Presence of God

These three stories can help us think about the relationship between suffering and the presence of God, his glory. A book which I have found helpful in thinking about this subject is *The Gospel of Glory*, by Richard Bauckham. It is a book about John's Gospel and many of the comments that follow are based on this book. You will recall that the term 'glory' often means more than simply honour and that it is often shorthand for those times when the invisible God becomes visible. Jesus continually radiated the glory of God and this was manifest in everything he did, both miracles and ordinary more mundane acts.

The glory of God in the Old Testament was often attended with dazzling splendour. Moses met God on a mountain surrounded by fire and thunder. Isaiah was overwhelmed with his sinfulness when he saw the Lord 'high and lifted up' in the Temple (Isaiah 6:1-5). We see the same thing in the life of Jesus when on the Mount of Transfiguration. His appearance was changed and his splendour was revealed to the three disciples who accompanied him. These were visual experiences, but also auditory: Moses glimpsed God, but then heard his voice (Exodus 34:6). On the Mount of Transfiguration (visual) the disciples heard the voice of God (auditory) and when Jesus performed miracles, the glory of God was revealed visually (John 2:11; 11:40 and 11:4).

But here is the surprising thing: the place where God's glory was most clearly seen was the Cross. God's glory was most perfectly revealed in and through suffering. In John 12:32 we read the words of Jesus 'when I am lifted up from the earth, I will draw all people to myself' and this follows God's stated intention to glorify his name through Jesus. The Cross, not just the resurrection, is the place where God is truly revealed, demonstrating the depth of love that the Father has for us. As Richard Bauckham writes, 'it is (Jesus') degradation and death, in the light of the resurrection, that constitutes the ultimate manifestation of God's glory'. Jesus went on to quote Isaiah 53 where a suffering servant is described (John 12:38). The servant ends up so marred in appearance that most would never recognise that his suffering was the ultimate revelation of who God is. The three stories included in this chapter resonate with the fact that the Cross was the place where God's glory, his presence, was most fully revealed.

So if you are suffering currently, it doesn't mean that you have missed it, lacked faith or somehow have displeased God. Of course, there might be a reason why we are suffering, but usually, it is neither our fault nor a sign of God's displeasure. Paul refers to a thought-provoking concept in Colossians 1:24 when he writes 'I am filling up what is lacking in Christ's afflictions for the sake of his body, that is the Church'. Paul wasn't suggesting that he was dying for our sins. What he meant was that if we want others to experience God's presence and grace for themselves, then it will require sacrifice on our part, including suffering.

Cultivating God's presence is not hindered by our experiences of suffering, just the opposite. We are not disqualified by suffering, even though we may feel restricted. God can use us despite, or even because of, our limitations, our illnesses or any opposition we encounter. The paradox is that God's presence is revealed both through healing and through suffering. In times of suffering our values are tested; in times of suffering, we are sustained by our rhythm of prayer. God's presence is not just for times of smooth sailing, since we can know the power of the resurrection and the *koinonia* (fellowship or partnership) of his suffering in the most difficult of times (Philippians 3:10).

17

Parting Thoughts

Crossing the Border

My own particular journey took a new turn when my imagination was captured by the Celtic saints and by Celtic monasticism, both of which continue to intrigue many people today. As well as its spirituality, Celtic monasticism was also attractive to me in being a missional movement with lessons for our situation in the West. Because Celtic monastics sought to relate God to the everyday lives of the pagan population around them, their efforts to contextualise the Gospel makes them a good choice for study since we find ourselves in a similar missionary situation. This is particularly so in Europe where vague New Age beliefs mingle with radical atheism and ill-defined secular 'spirituality'. Others, such as Martin Robinson in his book *Rediscovering the Celts,* have written about the potential of the Celtic Church as a paradigm for fresh missional thinking.

I am pleased that two decades ago, despite my initial reservations, I listened to my wife's advice and turned aside to look further. It is only when we 'turn aside to see' that we have the chance of encountering God for ourselves in a new way (Exodus 3:3). In certain respects, exploring monastic spirituality has felt like exploring a new land where some things are familiar and others less familiar. It borders the land of my spiritual birth in Charismatic Evangelicalism, as well as bordering other church landscapes, but the language used and customs themselves are somewhat different.

As when actual countries are in view, we can just visit or we can decide to actually move to live there. While I certainly have not abandoned my roots, I feel as if I have crossed the border and that New Monasticism is now my home. One element of the Celtic approach to pilgrimage has been summed up in the phrase 'finding a place of resurrection'. The journey has as its destination the discovery of the place where we feel most alive in God. This imaginative way of looking at pilgrimage captures something of the journey of those of us who have found a home in monastic inspired spirituality. New Monasticism has become the overarching approach into which I have sought to integrate much of my earlier experience. In fact, it dovetails well with the evangelical emphasis on the word of God and the charismatic emphasis on the power of God. In that respect, it feels less like a departure for somewhere new and more like a way of bringing together the various strands of my previous experience under one roof.

The Current Scene

New Monasticism is now an established part of the Christian landscape in the West, where many people have visited or been influenced by New Monastic centres. In the UK these centres, especially those on the Celtic fringes, have become sites of personal renewal for Christians from many different church backgrounds. Denominational or other allegiances are subsumed beneath a common desire to draw closer to God. The movement has tended to bring together Christians from different traditions and streams in keeping with Jesus' prayer in John 17:21. Taize in France, established in the 1940s is one of the forerunners in this ecumenical approach. Brother Roger, who founded the community, was influenced by studying Benedict's Rule and members live according to a simple Rule. Despite being Protestant in origin, Taize was visited by Pope John XXIII. It has given rise to its own recognisable style of worship, widely used across many Christian traditions.

Even the most sceptical might admit that New Monasticism, at its best, has brought a certain seriousness to the pursuit of God's presence. Often this quest has simply resulted in the rediscovery of what has been normative for Christian living throughout the centuries. There might, for example, be a renewed commitment to stewardship (contextualising poverty), to marital fidelity and premarital continence (chastity) and a submission to Scripture and inclusion of accountability structures (obedience). This is highly beneficial, even though it is simply reaffirming what is required of every disciple, rather than introducing something more radical; in that sense, it is not 'New' as such, since stewardship, fidelity and submitting to Scripture are in any case necessary. But it is 'New' in the sense that the words used to describe these aspects of discipleship are new and fresh *to our ears.*

The word 'New' in the phrase New Monasticism applies more directly if we adopt practices that are actually *new to us* such as a rhythm of prayer and a Rule of Life. When we think of the word 'monasticism', using examples of actual monks and nuns, such as those found in Celtic monasticism, may be a better catalyst for change than our adopting a set of monastic values - values can easily become somewhat idealistic or theoretical. Actual examples, by contrast, work more deeply by capturing our imagination; they help us to see what embodied truth looks like in reality.

What's Missing?

If this book were aimed at an academic audience it would have been appropriate to delve more deeply into the historical evidence for the existence of the Celts as a distinct group, as well as to consider more fully the question as to whether we can identify something called the Celtic Church. For readers interested in exploring this further a good starting point would be the writings of Ian Bradley and Donald Meek. Because their views are somewhat opposing it is worth considering them in tandem to give a more fully orbed perspective.

Again, if this had been a more academic work the concept of religious experience as a source of knowledge about God would have been discussed more thoroughly. Experience is one source of knowledge alongside Scripture, reason and the tradition of our particular branch of Christianity. I have assumed that the majority of readers will accept that the experience of God's presence is an authentic source of the knowledge of God. We need discernment in the way we interpret specific experiences that we or others have. This process can range from what in academia is known as critical thinking to the New Testament's idea of testing or discerning the spirits. So-called 'Critical Realism' is the approach adopted here - this affirms that there is a reality behind the experience of us all, but whether that reality is psychological, spiritual or arises from something else should be open to examination. This is particularly important when influential Christian leaders base their teaching mainly on personal experience.

New Monasticism vs Traditional Monasticism

The differences between traditional monasticism and engagement with monastic-inspired-spirituality will be somewhat evident from the earlier chapters. As well as these differences, our motivation for engaging with the New Monastic movement often differs from the motivation of those who join an enclosed monastic order. The idea of withdrawal from 'the world' to form a separated, self-sufficient, community contained within the walls of the monastery has its origins in those first monks who withdrew deep into the Egyptian desert. Those interested in New Monasticism frequently have almost the opposite impulse to that of the Desert Fathers and Mothers. We are seeking a set of practices, a way of life, which enables us to engage more fully with God in the context of our career, family and neighbourhood. New Monasticism is orientated towards becoming more deeply engaged with our communities and the wider world, rather than being oriented towards withdrawal from the world around us (although, of course, it necessarily involves times of withdrawal spent in prayer, meditation and reflection as part of its daily and annual rhythms). This is why the topics explored in the chapters on People, Proximity and Place are so important, as renewed engagement in these areas is central to the long-term effectiveness of this new movement.

For many Christians today finding a balance between more inwardly-focused practices (contemplation) and action is a challenge. Many traditional religious orders have members who lead busy lives outside the monastery, teaching or caring for the poor; they also seek to find a similar balance between action and contemplation. Celtic monasteries fostered engagement with those living outside their walls, both by inviting others in (providing places of retreat and hospitality) and by going out into their surrounding communities. But, in contrast to many of us today, times of intense activity were often punctuated by prolonged periods where individuals could withdraw to seek God's presence. This is a more realistic and more sustainable approach than expecting continual high-intensity engagement with people. A rhythm of engagement and withdrawal is something we ourselves might consider.

We have also noted that there is a similarity between New Monasticism and monastic orders in incorporating people who do not have the motivation or capacity to become full community members. These people join with the life of the monastery, but do not take full monastic vows or live the 'religious life'. People become Benedictine Oblates or Third Order Franciscans because they have a strong desire to live according to the values and practices of the order. They adopt selected aspects of the monastic life and work these through in their context, guided and supported by a spiritual director. Such an example in seeking support and advice can be followed and learned from by those within New Monastic circles so that we do not become isolated as we seek to outwork a Rule. Indeed, in some New Monastic circles, people are increasingly benefitting from the insights which spiritual direction can bring.

Finding a New Way

The suggestion of adopting a Rule may be an idea whose time has come. Following the Covid-19 pandemic, we have spent more time at home than ever before. This has thrown us back on our own company and on God. We have had a period of enforced withdrawal, and as one blogging monk wrote 'Covid has made monks of us all'. Many will continue to work from home, further reinforcing these trends. The example of monastic spirituality might, therefore, become more relevant than ever, as we seek fresh ways to inhabit our new and different world.

The importance of place, our neighbours and locality, has been both highlighted and strengthened. As a consequence of the Covid-19 pandemic, more people have been attending local food banks while some have got to know their neighbours for the first time. Others of us have had to take long local walks, rather than a holiday in the Mediterranean or Florida, opening our eyes literally to the physical environment around us. Within this new landscape, New Monasticism offers a way forward, outlining constructive ways to live in relationship with others. We discover effective ways to pray for the people around us and learn to speak blessing over our homes, streets and places of work. Adopting a Rule can (and should) include a commitment to be firmly rooted in our local Christian community, even if under normal circumstances we travel extensively with our work or ministry.

There are two further potential benefits of adopting a Rule. One is that it creates opportunities to hear God's voice, but without prescribing how he ought to speak to us. A gentle impression, a sense of being held or a dramatic experience are just some possibilities. It is easy in charismatic circles to associate God's presence mainly with one type of experience. People will drive long distances to attend a meeting where they hope to recapture a transformative experience which had been highly significant to them in their past. Similarly, when a strong presence of God has been reported in a particular place, such as a retreat centre, people travel there, seeking that particular experience. Of course, this can be a genuine hunger for God's presence but it can also be a symptom of seeking experience by going from one 'centre of renewal' to the next. The result is that we mistakenly believe that our walk with God needs a constant top-up from external sources - we can, in effect, become addicts. The practices outlined in this book aim at something more consistent. We easily fail to listen for the still small voice of God, if we limit God to earthquake, wind and fire.

The second potential for a Rule is that it might address what some authors and many in church leadership regard as the most pressing issue for the Church in the West - the need to find ways in which to foster discipleship. Despite many books on this topic very few seem to point to an effective way for this aspiration to become reality. Being taught from the Bible is clearly important, but teaching in churches often tends towards the theoretical and sometimes lacks connection with real life. Too many sermons tell us what to do but not *how to* apply it to everyday life (what we 'should do' outweighs the 'how to'). Perhaps we need to redefine teaching as instruction in the art of living. Others suggest that mentoring or coaching might be the answer and while those things certainly help, what is really needed is more of a complete package - an integrated and holistic approach to discipleship formation.

Discipleship is important because it addresses the third aspect of the Great Commission of Matthew 28, 'teaching them to observe all I have commanded you'. Following Jesus definitely involves learning certain things but notice that it is not learning new concepts as much as *learning to observe certain practices*. Although there is an element of head knowledge to being a Christian the most important element is that we learn to live in ways which *embody* the teachings of Jesus. A Rule helps us do just that.

Celtic monasticism presents us with a way of life. Monasteries were places of formation where monks and nuns were shaped through the rhythm of prayer, the monastic rhythm of daily life and obedience to the Rule. Space has not permitted more than a cursory examination of the potential of a Rule in leadership formation, but it holds much promise. It serves as a way of creating leaders who thereby experience being shaped by the Gospel; a process of formation, something which they are expected to cultivate for others once in ministry. The task of spiritual formation is both crucial and central, yet often leaders are trained to provide certain religious goods and services and to manage churches which are, in effect, small businesses. Few people are created with the ability to competently tackle both formation and management.

The New Landscape

Without the use of a crystal ball (forbidden by Scripture), there are several possible futures for the movement known as New Monasticism, different trajectories which may be taken. The three which immediately suggest themselves are:

1. Selecting Specific Practices

The first possible long-term outcome, or trajectory, is that many people will adopt specific practices but without embracing a Rule. Perhaps the classic example of this is the rediscovery of ancient approaches to prayer and Bible reading by charismatic and evangelical Christians. This might, for example, be through being introduced to Lectio Divina, the use of silence in prayer or Ignatian-style imaginative meditation on biblical stories. Such approaches can be life-transforming for many; for others, they simply confirm what has always been done but have given them a language to describe the way in which they naturally already pray. I recall a prominent evangelical leader saying that he and his wife went on an Ignatian retreat and that his wife immediately felt at home using imaginative meditation. She had always read the Bible that way, but with a strict evangelical upbringing, had thought of herself as being unusual. This experience legitimised her natural way of approaching Scripture.

Going on retreat is another practice which is now fairly commonly adopted as a regular component of evangelical spirituality. In my younger day, a retreat always meant wall-to-wall talks, interspersed with large doses of caffeine. There were no actual retreat practices, with little time set aside for silence, personal Bible reading and enquiring of the Lord. This is changing but perhaps not enough - asking a group of evangelical leaders to indicate whether they have experienced a silent retreat will often see few hands raised.

Adopting a few selective monastic practices has personal benefit, but it is not really what is meant by New Monasticism, the heart of which is adopting a Rule. If we choose just one or two aspects of monastic spirituality we could end up with a pick-and-mix approach, with no core to our spiritual life. A more integrated approach requires a core, a backbone, to bring together different elements to form a whole. We could, for instance, integrate some monastic practices into our existing evangelical spirituality (and many evangelicals have never considered the fact that they have a particular spirituality), in which case, evangelical spirituality is the stable core. In this event, we might end up having a traditional quiet time, attending a home-group for Bible study and regular Sunday worship - but we would supplement this by using Lectio Divina as our preferred method of Bible reading in our quiet time. This particular monastic practice dovetails well with our existing spirituality. Such an approach can be very productive, but when monastic inspired spirituality as a whole rather than just the adoption of specific practices is in view, we end up on a somewhat different journey; perhaps one of those outlined below.

2. Creating Parallel Structures

The second possible trajectory is that we might create parallel structures, alongside or in tandem with our existing church affiliation. These structures become the vehicle through which the practices of New Monasticism are reinforced. This approach has some similarities to that of Benedictine Oblates and Third Order Franciscans, who work out the implications of their vows in 'normal life'. The Northumbria Community has taken this route, with dispersed community members who meet regularly in local groups and who attend the 'motherhouse' in Northumbria for regular and annual retreats.

A similar but distinct move has been made by Ffald y Brenin in creating its Local Houses of Prayer network (LHOPs). This provides training, networking and a framework for prayer which has emerged from the experience of the retreat centre. Inspired by Celtic Christianity, certain practices, such as regularly speaking blessing, are integral to the LHOP approach. Ffald y Brenin's LHOPs have been established in every inhabited continent (www.localhousesofprayer.org).

Recognising the propensity of Evangelicals to simply follow the latest trend, much effort goes into presenting LHOPs as a set of values and practices which aim to cultivate God's presence. An emphasis on underpinning values means that this is not primarily a programmatic approach or the latest 'how-to' manual; it is not the latest bandwagon. There is no formal Rule at the time of writing, although the rhythm of prayer and other LHOP practices would articulate well with a Rule. Some of those involved also follow the Ffald y Brenin Rhythm of Daily Prayer, further reinforcing a connection to what might be equated with the 'motherhouse' of traditional monasticism.

Perhaps at this point, a word of caution is also necessary. There is always the danger of becoming enamoured with a dispersed community to the extent that it displaces face-to-face involvement in local church and community. A dispersed community can become a bubble world. This can be more attractive than the 'real world' since real interaction with others through the actual challenges and nitty-gritty of our lives is limited.

I have friends who help lead an acknowledged Anglican religious community called Hopeweavers. The community describe themselves as 'a dispersed fellowship of friends who seek God through silence and stillness, prayer, creativity, conversation and food, sharing the ups and downs of life wherever we are called to live and work'. They could be described as a New Monastic dispersed community. Although the Community of Hopeweavers takes up time and energy, there is synergy with their involvement in both church and their local community - Hopeweavers fosters the cultivation of practices which help sustain and nurture this involvement. Our friends run retreats in their home, some for Hopeweavers members and others that are open to non-members. They have also introduced contemplative practices into worship in their locality. This is a good example of how New Monasticism can help renew spiritual life where we live.

3. Forming Residential Communities

The third possibility is that residential communities based on a Rule of Life might take shape. In a culture where many people now live alone, this option could become increasingly attractive. This has already happened in a limited way in the UK, but more prominent examples known to me come from outside New Monastic circles. The European Network of Communities (ENC) is a body which involves 8,000 people from across Europe, including from within the UK. Individuals involved make a clear commitment to their particular community and some have embraced voluntary celibacy.

ENC communities represent a mix of residential houses and people living close to one another. Many of these communities are either Catholic or ecumenical and some have a specific focus, such as providing accommodation for the poor. In terms of influence, these sorts of communities out-punch their weight. The ENC sees itself as being neither a church nor a new religious order. They describe themselves as constituting a 'third way'.

The development of a greater number of residential centres, networked with other similar centres, is one possible trajectory for New Monasticism. I have regular contact with the 40-year-old Alleluia Community in Augusta Georgia. This group consists of 800 married and single people, lay and clergy, from various denominations and several aspects of community life are reminiscent of Celtic monasticism. They live near one another, having refurbished numerous semi-derelict properties in what was once a very poor area of their city. After a probationary period, new members join the community for life, similar to the Benedictine vow of stability. The area where they live is called Faith Village and my first visit to this community made me think of the Celtic monasterium, although Alleluia would not describe itself as New Monastic. Don Swenson, a Canadian sociology professor, in his published study of this community, compared it with the Essene settlement, an early monastic-styled community at Qumran which existed in the time of Jesus. While these sorts of communities, whether Catholic or ecumenical, might not have set out with the specific aim of reintegrating aspects of monastic practice into their life together, nevertheless, from the outside it appears that they do so to good effect.

Personal Engagement

New Monasticism is just one way, among many, of making ourselves more available to God. It is one approach to cultivating God's presence in our lives and neighbourhoods. We each relate to this 'monastic inspired spirituality' in a number of different ways and we may perhaps already be able to see where we fit within its rubric. We may, for example, simply be an interested observer, or we might already have adopted or want to adopt certain practices. We may even have decided to engage with it more thoroughly and want to embrace, or already have embraced, a Rule of Life. None of these positions, these current ways of engagement with New Monasticism, is static - change will occur as more is discovered and uncovered along our way.

Personal change is facilitated by three related but distinct processes. We can change through acquiring knowledge; this is *information* and it is important as it *informs* us about our faith. Being well-informed enables us to act wisely whenever we have choices to make. Information helps us to be grounded in reality, which is clearly important in an era of fake news. *Formation* is the second process which effects change - this involves adopting routines which gradually build character - they *form* us. A Rule of Life is a means to bring about formation. But there is a further process of change which also relates to the theme of this book;

that of *transformation* - cultivating God's presence *transforms* our lives. His glory touches our inner core in profound ways and the outcome is that we are unlikely to remain unchanged. All three - information, formation and transformation - are important, but it is the transformation of our lives from one degree of glory to another which most clearly enables others to see a reflection of the life of God.

A name that is often mentioned when the term New Monasticism is used is that of Dietrich Bonhoeffer. He famously wrote to his brother Karl Friedrich,

> The restoration of the Church will surely come from a sort of new monasticism which has in common with the old only the uncompromising attitude of a life lived according to the Sermon on the Mount in the following of Christ. I believe it is now the time to call people to this.

Bonhoeffer envisaged a restoration, or perhaps we could say a re-formation, of the Church that would profoundly change the Christian landscape. It could be that this new form of monasticism, already part of the Christian landscape in the West, will continue to gather momentum and widen its scope further afield, renewing and revitalising many from different Christian traditions and streams, increasingly drawing us together in unity.

Such a radical movement can only happen as we each embrace a new way of living. In the words of Charles Whitehead in the Foreword to this book, 'We all need a pattern of living which will enable us to dwell in God's presence and to be continually re-formed in his image. We all need practices whereby we might ourselves be transformed'. Could it be that we ourselves become the means by which 'the earth shall be filled with the glory of God as the waters cover the sea'*?*

... for Christ plays in ten thousand places,
Lovely in limbs, and lovely in eyes not his
To the Father through the features of men's faces.
GERARD MANLEY HOPKINS (AS KINGFISHERS CATCH FIRE)

About the Author

Richard lives in a small town in West Dorset, in the Southwest of England. He is married to Norma and they have three adult children and eight grandchildren. He is never happier than when he is near a river in some remote location with a fishing rod in hand. He is an amateur guitarist who has played many genres, but now sticks to playing his first love, the Blues.

Richard has a medical background in General Practice (family medicine) and psychotherapy. As part of Masters degrees in Counselling and in Theology he has researched Christian counselling practice and also the topic of Martin Luther King's relationship to the biblical prophets.

He has been involved in leadership in New Charismatic Church circles for 35 years and has also worked in theological education, having been director of studies for a Masters degree in Missional Leadership. He and Norma have planted two rural churches, including their current home-based church, The Meeting Place.

Richard is a trustee for the International Charismatic Consultation (formerly ICCOWE) and at Ffald y Brenin retreat centre in Wales. He is on the organising committee for the Gathering in Holy Spirit (Rome) and the Charismatic Leaders Fellowship (USA). Since 2012 he has been involved in official Conversations between the New Charismatic Churches (non-denominationals) and the Pontifical Council for Promoting Christian Unity in Rome. These involvements have resulted in many valued friendships and a growing awareness of the potential for Christians from different Church traditions to enrich one another's lives.

His recent publications include *The Characteristics of the New Charismatic Churches*, available on the Vatican website, and an article entitled *Networked Church: Theological, Sociological and Historical Perspectives* published in the journal *Pneuma*.

The author's website: www.newcharismatic.com